RARE BOOK
LIBRARIANSHIP

RARE BOOK
LIBRARIANSHIP

Roderick Cave

CLIVE BINGLEY
LONDON

LINNET BOOKS
HAMDEN   CONN

FIRST PUBLISHED 1976 BY CLIVE BINGLEY LTD
16 PEMBRIDGE ROAD LONDON W11
SIMULTANEOUSLY PUBLISHED IN THE USA BY LINNET BOOKS
AN IMPRINT OF THE SHOE STRING PRESS INC
995 SHERMAN AVENUE HAMDEN CONNECTICUT 06514
SET IN 10 ON 13 POINT BASKERVILLE
PHOTOSET, PRINTED AND BOUND IN GREAT BRITAIN BY
REDWOOD BURN LTD TROWBRIDGE AND ESHER
COPYRIGHT ⊙ RODERICK CAVE 1976
ALL RIGHTS RESERVED
BINGLEY ISBN 0-85157-180-8
LINNET ISBN 0-208-01360-1

For Dawn

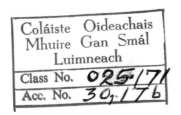
Library of Congress Cataloguing in Publication Data

Cave, Roderick.
    Rare book librarianship.

    Bibliography: p.
    Includes index.
    1. Libraries—Special collections—Rare books. I. Title.
Z688.R3C38   025.17'1   75-29045
ISBN 0-208-01360-1

Contents

List of illustrations

Preface

Although there is an extensive and enjoyable literature on the subject of rare books, most of it is concerned with bibliography or book collecting, and relatively little on the *librarianship* of rare books is available. This book is an attempt to consider some of the problems of custodianship and exploitation of special collections in libraries: problems sufficiently different, I believe, to make the concept of rare book librarianship a valid one. It is based distantly upon lecture notes for a course on this subject which was offered to postgraduate students at Loughborough University.

The writer's own interests are centred around the history of printing. An apology is perhaps due for the fact that a larger proportion of the examples given are drawn from this field than from English literature, the history of science, or other areas of learning in which rare book collections are of particular importance. No doubt there are other instances in which personal interests and preferences are obvious. It is perhaps worth stating that references to what is now the British Library Reference Division as the British Museum is not an indication of reactionary cussedness: since most of the publications and services of this institution which are discussed in the text are from the period before the British Library was created, it seemed appropriate consistently to use the older name.

It is normal for a writer to acknowledge the help he has received from others. In this case it is not just a formal courtesy: as I have been in the West Indies for the past few years I have had to call on help from others to a greater extent than usual, and without the help I have received by correspondence and otherwise this book could not have been written. I am particularly grateful to John Aarons, Paul Banks, Nicolas Barker, Terry Belanger, Clinton Black, William J Cameron, Georges Colin, Philip Gaskell, Hans Halbey, Andrew Horn, F G B Hutchings, K E Ingram, Bill Jackson, Herman Liebaers, Jackson

MacWilliams, Roy Stokes, Michael Turner, Derek Warren and James Wells. For the illustrations, the Bibliothèque Royale, Brussels, the Jamaica Archives, and the Klingspor Museum, Offenbach-a-M have been very helpful. My thanks are due also to the Antiquarian Booksellers Association and to the Rare Books Group of the Library Association for permission to include a part of their joint report on book thefts from libraries as an appendix.

The errors of omission and commission are my own.

Roderick Cave
Irish Town, Jamaica

Chapter 1
Introduction

Many librarians, in many different types of library, have had the experience of the reader who comes into their library carrying a large, carefully wrapped volume, whose antiquity and probable monetary value is a matter of family legend. Reverently revealed for inspection, it turns out to be a nineteenth-century bible, with leaves foxed and in a decaying leather binding. It is emphatically *not* a rare book destined to make the family's fortune in the auction rooms; and the librarian has the unenviable task of explaining to the disbelieving reader that the book's association or sentimental value to the family is likely to be far higher than its market price.

Because of this popular conception of the rare book, which many of us share to some extent, of a precious volume, a bibliographical curiosity—perhaps a forty-two line bible, or a first folio of Shakespeare, or a Kelmscott Chaucer, safely locked in an exhibition case and certainly not resting on the shelves of our own library—many librarians prefer to avoid using the phrase 'rare books' and instead to speak of 'special collections' when describing material under their care.

The terminology is not particularly important, as long as it is recognised that we are dealing with a special category of library materials (which of course need not be books) whose acquisition, technical processing, storage and exploitation all call for different treatment from the run-of-the-mill stock of the library. The material need not be old, nor rare (in the strict sense of the term as used by the book collector) nor command a high market price. Indeed the individual item once separated from the collection of which it forms a part may be utterly negligible. Essentially, however, it will be material for which the librarian assumes his oldest role as *custodian*: material which is being treated differently from the rest of the stock not only because of the need to exploit it for use but because of the duty to preserve it for the future. In this book the terms 'rare books' and 'special collections' are used interchangeably in this sense of custodianship, although of course some of the topics dealt with in succeeding chapters have more relevance for the books which are old and uncommon and expensive than for those which are modern, cheap and in good supply.

The nature of the special collection will naturally vary considerably from library to library, and within a single institution there is likely to be a number (perhaps a large number) of collections of this sort which call for special handling. Local history collections are one of the commonest varieties, to be found almost everywhere. Colleges of education may accumulate specimens of textbooks, of early books for children and so forth, which will form a distinct part of the library. An art school which offers courses in printing or graphic design is likely over the years to build up a collection of specimens of fine printing which will require different housing and handling from the general stock of its library. In universities special collections which provide in depth for the research needs of staff and postgraduate students will develop naturally out of the university's work. When a locality is particularly associated with a certain trade or industry, it is natural for the libraries concerned to extend their local collections so that they become especially rich in the literature of that trade.

In many instances, the mere passage of time will mean that some books in a library's collections need to be transferred from the open shelves to the rare book room so that their physical care and preservation for posterity can be ensured. The library of a professional association or learned society founded in the nineteenth century is likely to be rich in this sort of material To give one example, the joint library of the Iron and Steel Institute and the Institute of Metals, even without its purposeful collecting of early metallurgical literature has acquired many books and pamphlets which the passage of time has made of particular interest for the history of technology, and which call for special attention.

Unlike some of the more affluent libraries of North America, which may in their quest for excellence set out deliberately to build up rare book collections from scratch, British libraries today seldom have the opportunity for such development. Their special collections have come in a different way. Frequently this will have been by the deposit,

10

gift or bequest of private collections (which is also, of course, the more typical development in American libraries). The Parkes Library at Southampton University, which is concerned with Jewish studies, is an example. Another is the John Johnson collection of printed ephemera now in the Bodleian; the late Barry Ono's collection of 'penny dreadfuls' (on which Louis James drew so heavily for his *Fiction for the working man*) in the British Museum is a third. Such collections are not only to be found in large research libraries, of course: the eighteenth-century parish libraries of Loughborough and Ashby de la Zouche now housed and maintained in Loughborough Technical College are further instances of rare book collections in a library of modest size.

All this is commonplace, and one would think hardly needed saying. Yet there are sufficient horror stories that one hears, about the way in which rare and perhaps irreplaceable books are treated by those charged with their care, to make it quite obvious that today it is still possible and even reasonable to regard librarians as enemies of books, to adopt the title of a paper written thirty years ago by the late Randolph G Adams.(1)

I am not now referring to the theft of books, plates, maps and so on, about which one hears a good deal. The most scrupulously administered collection is subject to this curse, and in a sense the greater the library the more it is at risk.(2) Rather it is the wanton and illegal dispersal of parish libraries by those supposed to be their custodians,(3) or the newspaper reports of the sale of a library's stockroom to an antiquarian bookseller for £10 instead of the £200 which was nearer its market value,(4) or the incident in which another public library very nearly sent a substantial collection of eighteenth century books in original bindings to a firm of library binders to be reclothed in neat modern dress.(5) When librarians treat rare books in this way, they have no need of other enemies.

That librarianship's professional associations, almost as much in the United States as in Britain, have been relatively little concerned with the problems of rare book librarianship is largely a matter of historical accident. The essentially utilitarian purpose of the public library movement in the late nineteenth century, with the emphasis placed upon open access and positive service by the leaders of the profession in the public library field, tended naturally to put them out of sympathy if not actually at odds with those librarians whose work was for the few and whose collections were necessarily closed to general public access.

It was not entirely a matter of professional differences on function, nor of a different philosophy of service. It was partly a social difference; one of class. The librarian in a rare book collection was perhaps too mandarin in attitude, and certainly too little concerned with explaining the nature of his work and the purpose behind it to the outsider, for much understanding of his duties to be shown by those principally concerned with education for librarianship in the early part of this century. However much one cares for rare books oneself, one can feel considerable sympathy for such forward-looking librarians as James Duff Brown and the irritation he expressed with the work of the Bibliographical Society in his paper in *The library* in 1903.(6) The gentlemanly mauling which Brown received in the same issue,(7) though well-merited, did little to reduce the widening gap between keepers of rare books and the mainstream of professional librarianship.

In the United States the situation was very much the same. There were of course fewer old-established institutional libraries containing large collections of rare materials than in Britain at the time professional librarianship began to organise itself, but in some of these the old concept of the librarian-scholar and librarian-collector remained pre-eminent. With the emergence of rare book departments in the growing university libraries (and the University of Michigan set up its rare book room as long ago as 1899) and above all the creation by public spirited book-collectors of totally new libraries devoted very largely to rare materials—the John Carter Brown Library in 1904, the Huntington in 1920, the Pierpont Morgan in 1924 are but a few—the gulf between rare book librarianship and professional librarianship widened: ... 'High on the list of reasons [for the separate establishment of these research libraries] was a thoroughgoing distrust of the dehumanising aspects of professional librarianship. In selecting their librarians and curators the benefactors usually consciously

12

avoided the 'professional librarian' and chose men and women who were sympathetic with the humanistic and bibliophilistic motives behind their collections . . . to carry on the humanistic traditions of librarianship.

Between the two world wars these men and women began to raise their kind of librarianship to a new eminence. Standing between the library and scholarly professions they partook a little of each . . . As librarians outside the profession they freely criticised it for its shortcomings. They stressed the failure to care properly for books, the concentration on service in terms of quantity rather than quality, the growing library bureaucracy with its committees and conferences and the somewhat self-conscious preoccupation with professionalism.'(8)

To a considerable extent the family quarrel between the branches of library work has declined. The governors of a learned library may in 1976 advertise that they are looking for a scholar and not a professional librarian—but in most rare book collections you will now find at least some of the staff with professional librarianship training among their other qualifications. The rare books librarians may still prefer meetings of the Bibliographical Society, or the Bibliographical Society of America, to those of library associations—but the Library Association now has a lively Rare Books Group, and some of the pre-conference sessions on rare books organised by ACRL make the American Library Association's annual meetings of more value. Rare book librarianship may still not figure very largely in the preoccupations of those concerned with education for library work—but some consideration of some of the problems of special collections will be included in most library schools' syllabuses, while at the same time the level of education of professional librarians is higher, so that people from research libraries will meet and share common ground with those from other types of library to an extent that was certainly not true even fifteen years ago.

Nevertheless, despite the closing of the gap between these branches of librarianship, changing concepts of the librarian's role in society are producing their own dangers. With the application of cost benefit analysis and other sophistications in library management, with the increase in library automation and ideas of computer

13

storage of information, with fashionable talk of libraries as learning resource centres, and (above all) with the stresses caused by the ever increasing rate of publicaction, the extra attention given to rare books is necessarily limited, and often outweighed by such matters. In practice, often no more than lip-service is paid to the function of the librarian as the keeper (in Archibald MacLeish's words) of 'the records of the human spirit', and there is a very real danger that the development of new services in the library will be at the expense of its earlier role.

To quote one example, James Thompson in his *Introduction to university library administration*(9) is by no means unsympathetic to rare books or their place in a university library. However, his comment on the Parry Report's statement that 'It is not proper to subsidise from public funds a desire to acquire items simply because they are bibliographical curiosities' is an interesting one. 'This really cannot be contested'; he wrote, 'and there was certainly an unfortunate tendency in university libraries during their "storehouse" period of development to indulge in this type of acquisition, *which in merit ranks no higher than collecting postage stamps.*' (My italics).

That books exist which are no more than 'bibliographical curiosities' I have no doubt, nor that the Parry Committee and Mr Thompson have a clear idea of the nature of such things. If the University of Barset buys an incunable simply in order to possess one fifteenth century book, the incunable will be a bibliographical curiosity with value only as a sort of museum exhibit, and not as a book to be consulted. Obviously it cannot be contested (as Mr Thompson has it) that such a purchase would be improper—are we not all against Sin?—but the difficulty lies in defining 'bibliographical curiosities'. This sort of criticism was levelled at Folger's assiduous collecting together of first folios. It *was* remarkably like collecting postage stamps, and how valuable it was to scholarship, and how wrong the critics were, Charlton Hinman's work on the printing and proofreading of the first folio has shown beyond any doubt.

The real danger, to be sure, is not from those in the library profession, whether they are curators of rare book collections or not. There was an interesting passage in the *San Francisco chronicle* of 9

November 1971: 'A Reagan administration report has recommended that the University of California can "Beat inflation" by offering its rare books and special book collections for auction. "Most of these collections were acquired before the market for rare books was so large" said the confidential report now being circulated in the University "and they could be sold at a tremendous profit".(10) Naturally the authorities of the University of California were resisting this recommendation, and the State Government was treating this resistance indulgently: '"It's the difference possibly between the libraries' approach to what the library ought to be and a businessman's approach" said Bill Berriesford, senior management auditor of the State Department of Finance.' When the 'Businessman's approach' is adopted all rare books become merely bibliographical curiosities. The dangers inherent for librarianship in such an approach need no explanation.

References

1 Randolph G Adams, 'Librarians as enemies of books' *Library quarterly*, vol 7 1937 pp 317–31.

2 The best known modern instance is probably T J Wise's removal of leaves from the British Museum's copies of pre-restoration dramatists under the noses of the staff in the North Library, so well described by David Foxon in his *Thomas James Wise and the pre-restoration drama* (London, Bibliographical Society, 1959). The literature of book thefts is of course extensive, and often of considerable interest and importance in rare book librarianship. An excellent though dated survey is Lawrence S Thompson's 'Notes on bibliokleptomania' *Bulletin of the New York Public Library* Sept 1944; subsequently included in William Targ, *Carrousel for bibliophiles* New York, Duschnes, 1947; reprinted Metuchen NJ, Scarecrow Press, 1967 pp 94–143.

3 A horrifying account of depredations in the past generation was given on pp 57–9 of the Central Council for the Care of Churches' *The parochial libraries of the Church of England* London, Faith Press, 1959.

4 *Library Association record* January 1973, p 14.

5. Quoted from personal knowledge. What was so disturbing about this instance was that the librarian concerned had no idea whatsoever

15

that the eighteenth century bindings, bookplates, inscriptions on end-leaves etc were of the slightest importance.

6 *The library* 2nd series, vol 4 1903, pp 144–51.

7 By A W Pollard of the British Museum, op cit pp 151–62.

8 Thomas R Adams, 'Rare books: their influence on the library world', *Library quarterly* vol 5 no 4 (April 1957) pp 426–33.

9 London, Bingley; Hamden, Conn, Linnet Books 1970. The passage quoted is on page 59.

10 Quoted in the *Book collector* vol 21 1972 p 410, from which the account given above has been taken.

Chapter II
The nature of the rare book

To the scholar or student the nature of a rare book is a simple matter; it is one which he wishes to consult and cannot get easily from a library or bookshop. A slightly more sophisticated definition will mention that such books are not handled through the usual channels for the purchase of new books, whether library supplier or bookseller, but instead must be bought (when they can be bought at all) through specialist dealers, auction houses and the like.

Additions to the special collections in a library are different from the rest of the stock in precisely this way, that the vast majority of acquisitions will be of materials which are not in print and cannot be obtained through the library's normal sources of supply, whereas for the other departments of a library although out-of-print material may and will be obtained—back sets of periodicals spring to mind as a typical example—it is unlikely to form more than a small proportion of acquisitions for those departments.

In the special collection one is dealing, essentially, with second-hand books, and in precisely the same way as in the purchase of any other second-hand objects, the rules of the game are quite different from those for the purchase of new. When one is buying a new book there is little difference whether one obtains it from any library supplier of one's choice, the price remains the same in any case. If on the other hand it is a secondhand book which one is buying, totally different methods are appropriate: there is no net price, but only a market average which will probably be difficult to ascertain in many cases. The different copies which come on to the market will vary in condition: one may be immaculate as published, another somewhat worn, a third heavily used but bear an inscription in the author's hand, and so forth. The prices asked will naturally differ for each copy.

Within the antiquarian book trade (a term which for convenience I shall use to mean all the trade sources, from junkshop to distinguished auction house, which one may use to purchase materials for special collections) there are many factors which will affect the way a particular book is handled and which cause a particular price to be established for any given item. These factors, central to the nature of the rare book and of course interdependent in their effect, are those of RARITY, REPUTATION (of book or author), FASHION, CONDITION, and PROVENANCE.

Rarity

There is an abundance of definitions in the literature of book-collecting of the nature of rarity, and also of attempts to introduce some sort of order or logic into an area full of subjective judgments. John Hill Burton, in his now antiquated but still useful and readable *The book hunter* (London, 1862) quoted a dictum of David Clement, the eighteenth-century French bibliographer, that 'a book which it is difficult to find in the country where it is sought ought to be called simply *rare*; a book which is difficult to find in any country may be called *very rare*; a book of which there are only fifty or sixty copies existing, or which appears so seldom as to suggest that there never had been more at any time than that number of copies, ranks as *extremely rare*; and when the whole number of copies does not exceed ten, this constitutes *excessive rarity*, or *rarity in the highest degree*.' Utter pedantry, commented Burton, and so it is since it ignores the essential factor that unless books are sought for (whether by collectors, acquisitions librarians or by scholars) their actual rarity is a matter of no importance whatsoever: there are plenty of books which according to Clement's definition are *rare in the highest degree* and yet would never find a buyer.

Rarity was naturally touched upon by the eminent bibliographer A W Pollard in the article on book-collecting which he contributed to the eleventh edition of the *Encyclopaedia Britannica*. Book-collecting he defined as 'the bringing together of books which in their contents, their form or the history of the individual copy possess some element of permanent interest, and either actually or prospectively are rare, in the sense of being difficult to procure. This qualification of rarity, which figures much too largely in the popular view of book-collecting, is entirely subordinate to that of interest, for the rarity of a book devoid of interest is a matter of no concern. On the other hand, so long as a book (or anything else) is and appears likely to continue to be easily procurable at any moment, no one has any reason for collecting it. The anticipation that it will always be easily procurable is often unfounded; but so long as the anticipation exists it restrains collecting, with the result that horn-books are much rarer than first folio Shakespeares.' Despite Pollard's comment that rarity figured too largely in the popular conception, it remains one of the basic elements in book-collecting, and necessarily impinges upon the librarian. It is no mere coincidence that the institutions gathered together and so sympathetically described by Anthony Hobson in his *Great libraries* (London, 1970) are libraries which whether by historical accident or deliberate intention are particularly rich in rare books.

In his erudite, witty and perceptive series of Sandars Lectures given at Cambridge in 1947, later published as *Taste and technique in book collecting*,(1) John Carter analysed with care the different varieties of rarity in books.

Absolute rarity, as distinguished by Carter, is the property inherent in any book printed in an extremely small number of copies, and of which the number of potential survivors can therefore be estimated with accuracy. Carter mentions as an example the early nineteenth century collector Archdeacon Wrangham, whose tastes led him to have a few copies of his own publications pulled on coloured paper, a fad shared by other bibliophiles of the time.(2)

Other instances are of course to be found in some of the editions of books printed on vellum,(3) or some issues of the *livres d'artiste* in France or of private presses elsewhere. The Hammer Creek Press of New York, for instance, is reputed to print most of its work in editions of only two copies; the Officina Bodoni of Verona has on occasion produced equally small editions.

The deliberate creation of rarities has, perhaps, some appeal for the book-collector, but is obviously quite without merit from the librarian's point of view. In most cases, and for most purposes, the library's function can be performed quite adequately by obtaining the 'ordinary' editions rather than the special issues described above. Admittedly it might be desirable in particular cases to obtain the special issues: a collection devoted to or concerned with the work of the wood-engraver John Buckland Wright will be the poorer if it possesses the ordinary edition of *Mademoiselle de Maupin* published by the Golden Cockerel Press in place of the special issue, (4) since the latter contains four extra engravings omitted from the larger edition. Usually this will not be so, and the matter will be of concern to the librarian only because his collection has come into possession, by bequest or other accession, of a book or books which possess this attribute of absolute rarity.

The property may of course be extended to other works for which the number of copies printed was not deliberately restricted to such an extent, but for which historical accident has achieved the same result. The edition of Swift's *Selected essays* published by the Golden Cockerel Press in 1925 consisted nominally of 450 copies, but as a result of an accident in production only 190 copies were published. (5) Through a similar accident in binding, ninety of the hundred copies of Evelyn Ansell's *Twenty-five poems* (Vine Press, 1963) were damaged through off-setting of the ink, and though the situation was retrieved 'the only copies in perfect condition are the ten in full leather'. (6) A more extreme instance is that of Count Wofgang Bethlen's *History of Transylvania* which was nearing completion at his castle of Kreich when it was besieged and taken by the Turks, in 1697. When retaken from the Turks a century later, two copies of this book could be made up from the scraps found rotting in a cellar. (7)

The problem with books of this kind, of course, is that it is extremely hard to establish the absolute rarity of the material. With the examples quoted above it is a relatively simple matter since the facts (8) are readily accessible; in other instances—those editions the bulk of which were destroyed in the blitz, for example—it becomes much more a matter of conjecture than of established fact: one may suspect that certain books are *absolutely rare* but be able to establish only their *relative rarity*.

Relative rarity, the second of the categories distinguished by Carter, is not concerned directly with the size of the original edition, but instead with the survival of copies and (for the collector) the frequency with which they appear on the market. The first folio of Shakespeare, or the 42-line bible are instances of books which are not particularly rare in absolute terms, nor even relatively rare when one considers the total number of known copies: as Pollard said, first folios are commoner than horn-books. Yet, having been sought for by collectors over a long period of time, the chances of unrecorded copies turning up are not very great. The census of known copies is therefore a fairly accurate indication of the total to survive.

This is of course true (in so far as it is true) for celebrated 'high-spots' but far less so for the majority of books coming within the purview of the antiquarian book trade. The massive increases in the past few years in the market value of books concerned with the history of science and technology, for example, have brought back into circulation many volumes which previously languished almost forgotten in booksellers' storerooms or in private collections. *Temporary rarity* (another of Carter's categories) is a simple instance of the time lag in the antiquarian market's adjusting itself to new areas of demand like this. Only the passage of time will show whether the present scarcity of a certain book on, say, bridge-building, is because the work is genuinely rare or whether on the other hand it is merely temporarily uncommon, and higher market prices will bring out a sufficiently large number of copies from their present obscurity to satisfy the demand.

Local rarity is another factor of importance, particularly in regard of the minor material which makes up so large a proportion of most special collections. Simply expressed, it means that unless a book has attracted bibliophilic attention over a long period of time (as with the editions of Aldus, for instance) copies of it are more likely to be found in the area of original circulation than elsewhere. The publications of the clandestine presses in occupied Holland during the second world war will naturally be found more frequently in the Netherlands than elsewhere. Such localised rarity is affected in time by attention paid to the material outside its area of natural circulation: because these clandestine presses have received some attention in Britain and the United States(9) there has been a small drift of copies of their books

21

into the English book trade, but it remains true that such material is far rarer in Britain than in the Netherlands, and that the purposeful acquisition of Dutch underground printing can be undertaken much better in Amsterdam than in Oxford or Los Angeles.

Local rarity is a factor of importance in building up a collection, to be sure, but it has the compensation that books temporarily exiled may at times be purchased at prices considerably lower than obtains in their natural homes. I have been able to buy English books in the Netherlands and even in California at prices lower than those prevailing in London because the local demand for the books was less. Probably more often, alas, the reverse can be true and the price asked by a continental bookseller be higher than that prevailing in the English trade where the book is commoner.

In addition to these various types of rarity there are some factors which are of particular interest to the librarian. Those already discussed will obviously impinge upon the curator of a special collection as they will also upon the private collector.

It is a commonplace that the supply of rare books is drying up, and that it is beyond the realms of possibility for libraries to extend their collections in certain fields which they might wish to cultivate were there a reasonable chance of being able to obtain the books. The use of lithographic or other reprint editions, or of microfilms can of course meet many of the requirements of a research collection, as discussed below in Chapters VI and VIII, but this is a different matter. Of these special library factors of rarity one is concerned particularly with the supply of material. The value of a special collection lies less in its 'high-spots', important though they may be, than in the corpus of material of secondary value, some of which may be of very little market value or indeed actual rarity.

Carter mentions Bishop Stillingfleet's *Sermons* as being in the same unmarketable class of books as Victorian bibles, as indeed they may be although I suspect that they are less of a drug on the market than forty years ago, and certainly cannot easily be obtained without outlay any more. Victorian bibles, however, despite increased interest in victoriana are not by and large objects of commerce within the antiquarian book trade. Nor are mid-nineteenth century editions of

22

Shakespeare, yet to build up a collection of these is a function assumed by the Folger Library in Washington as a necessary concomitant to its other Shakespeare collections.

Much material appropriate for special collections, then, will not appear in the antiquarian book trade because the demand for it is insufficiently developed to make the cost of cataloguing and so forth worthwhile. This is *market rarity*, which will make many books much more difficult to procure (although cheaper when found) than material which has been within the scope of the trade for some time. Subsidiary editions, translations, and of course locally published material will frequently be the subject of market rarity of this kind; its market rarity may disguise the other factors of which Carter speaks, very effectively indeed.

Another consideration is a book's *rarity in institutional libraries*. Capperonier de Gauffecourt's *Traité de reliure* is a book absolutely rare in the strictest sense.(10) Though not a particularly good book, as the earliest separate publication on bookbinding it is of considerable interest and is often cited in the literature of the subject. The only copy in an institutional library that I have been able to trace is that in the Municipal Library of Dijon: the pressure of demand is therefore concentrated entirely on this copy.

Similarly scholarly consultation of particular rare books will be greater in those libraries which are well-known for their collections in the particular subject field, or whose ownership of copies is well publicized. In most cases the copies of sixteenth century books in Bodley or the British Museum will be more heavily used than, for instance, those copies surviving in Archbishop Marsh's Library in Dublin, or the Plume Library at Maldon; the copybooks of writing masters possessed by the Victoria and Albert Museum or the Newberry Library at Chicago will be more heavily used than other copies of the same books as students of the genre naturally gravitate towards those collections well known for their richness in the field.

The selective recording of libraries' holdings of rare books (in Wing, for example) of course has the effect that readers' use tends to become concentrated on the recorded copies rather than those not listed. This produces problems of two sorts for the curators of rare books collections: in the well used collection it intensifies the problem of conservation, and since books are for use it means also that the other under-utilised libraries have to make greater efforts than otherwise to publicise their holdings. Some of the methods by which this may be done are considered below, in Chapters IX and X. Rarity of this last sort, which could perhaps be described as 'Rarity in bibliographies and union lists', is of considerable importance in the establishment of prices: 'Not in Wing', 'STC has one location only in America', 'Unknown to Wagner-Camp' and similar phrases are familiar in booksellers' catalogues, where they are very reasonably used to establish a book's desirability.

To judge the rarity of a book is no easy matter, obviously; it is something which comes only as a result of years of experience working with the material. There are several different factors involved, which are discussed at length by Carter. (11) Summarised, these include:

1 The size of the original edition: other things being equal, more copies should survive of a large printing than of a small one.

2 Limited editions and the connoisseurs market: books which are deliberately produced for collectors (and, it may be added, books lavishly got-up and presentation copies) are much less liable to natural attrition than ordinary editions, from publication onwards normally being in the hands of those who appreciating their value(12) are unlikely to discard them.

3 The reputation of the book or author or publisher: books which from an early period in their life were highly esteemed and became collected will naturally have suffered less than books not so regarded. Bewick's engravings have always been well thought of, for example, and the survival of books with his illustrations is higher than for disregarded material of the same age. The corollary of course is that material regarded as ephemeral has proved to be so: theatre programmes, pamphlets and the like are much rarer than bound volumes, and it is only as the result of some early collectors' interest—Humphrey Dyson's proclamations, Thomason's civil war tracts—that some have survived at all. In modern terms one would naturally expect a greater proportion of paperbacks to disappear than of volumes in publishers' cases.

24

4 Rarity in 'collectors' state': in the case of fragile and easily damaged material, the number of surviving copies in fine state may be a far lower proportion of the total surviving copies than usual. For many of the purposes of a special collection, of course, a copy in somewhat less than collectors' condition may be quite adequate.

5 Publishers' standing: books from large, well-established firms will in general be commoner than those bearing minor imprints. Even with well-established firms, books on subjects outside their normal scope of operations, or books by authors most of whose work appeared under another imprint, will be relatively more uncommon than usual.

6 Authors' standing: in general, books by authors at the height of their careers will be easier to find than both those issued before they had established a reputation and those published when their star was on the wane.

7 Traditional rarity: once books have acquired the reputation of being rare (whether deserved or not) they acquire a much greater survival value than others possess.

Reputation and fashion

The reputation of a particular book, or of its author, naturally has a distinct effect on its market value. *Savrola* is by no stretch of the imagination a good novel, yet it commands a high price because it was written by Winston Churchill. Its high price, to be sure, derives in no small measure from its rarity compared with other books written by Churchill, but it serves as an excellent instance of a book which is regarded as worth collecting solely because of its author's reputation in other fields of endeavour. The history of publishing is full of such instances.

It is not usually the case that an author achieves great popular success or critical acclaim with his first book, but rather that he will build up to this gradually. The books for which he is well known will command a higher price, being more generally sought for, than either his 'prentice work or his books published when his reputation is in decline—a higher price, that is, in relation to their rarity. Trollope's first novel, *The MacDermots of Ballycloran*, is infinitely rarer than, say, *The last chronicle of Barset* or *Phineas Finn*, and its market value reflects this

25

rarity. But both *The last chronicle* and *Phineas Finn* are books for which the market price will be higher (relative to rarity, once more) than much of the work of Frances Trollope or Thomas Adolphus Trollope, the mother and elder brother of Anthony, because their novels though by no means negligible are not part of the established canon in the same way.

Similarly, the works of John Masefield are not to current critical or collecting tastes. Having in the nineteen-twenties and thirties been the subject of collecting at what one would now consider very fancy prices, his books can now be obtained for a very modest outlay. Yet although Masefield's work is now in the doldrums, his major books still command higher prices—as ever, in relation to rarity—than his minor work.

Critical fashion plays a very considerable part in settling ideas of the market value of books. It need not of course be the dictates of the literary establishment: Sheridan Le Fanu's novels and stories are an instance of the higher valuation that book collecting not infrequently places on minor literary figures. Yet critical esteem obviously plays its part in such cases also: *Hermsprong* is the only novel by Robert Bage in which any except PhD students in search of a thesis are likely to be interested, and though his other novels may be almost equally witty and amusing they are much less highly valued. Conan Doyle's historical romances are perhaps superior to the Sherlock Holmes volumes, but it is the latter which are sought.

Lists of 'significant' books were commonplace earlier in this century (the Grolier One Hundred, for instance) and had a considerable effect in guiding collecting fashions. The taste for such top-twentyish compilations is by no means dead today, as witness Cyril Connolly's *The modern movement*. They have their uses, not least to the bookseller.

Fashion guiding lists may not be as simple as this, of course. The selection of key books in western civilisation for the exhibition 'Printing and the mind of man' at Earl's Court and the British Museum in 1963, since so ably described in the book of the same title,(13) is an excellent example of the way in which the collecting of rare books can be channelled into a new direction. The exhibition and the book were not themselves responsible for the vast increase in the prices of books important in the history of science and technology; they were symptomatic of changes already taking place. Nevertheless, it is probably safe to say that the asking prices for books canonised by inclusion have appreciated in the past ten years more than for other books of perhaps equal importance in the field which were not so selected.

The arbitrary dictates of fashion may of course be turned to good advantage. The high regard in which incunabula have for long been held has obviously pushed prices for all fifteenth century books upwards very considerably, although for more than half a century scholars have recognised that 1520 is a more logical terminal date for the early period of printing than 1500. But because of these long-standing fashions, it was possible for a library or collector in the palmy days of the nineteen-thirties to form a significant collection of books published in the first twenty years of the sixteenth century at prices substantially lower than obtained for books of similar merit but published a few years earlier.(14) If one is on the other hand responsible for developing a collection in a subject area ·which becomes fashionable, of course, prices may well escalate to such an extent that one has to reconsider the future scope of the collection very carefully indeed.

Condition

Books in collectors' condition naturally command higher prices than those which are not regarded as achieving this. What constitutes collectors's condition is another matter, and varies a great deal with the period, the type of book and will be further influenced by the rarity of the book under consideration. The rules which collectors impose on themselves will naturally be less rigorous for books which are absolutely rare than for those of which there is an adequate supply.

In the abstract, one can say(15) that a book cannot normally be regarded as being in collectors' condition unless it is complete and undisturbed in its original binding or casing, and is clean and sound throughout. To demand this for a book by a contemporary author, expecting the dustjacket to be present and for there to be a degree of freshness about the physical state of the book is perfectly reasonable. With due modification for the freshness of the casing and contents, it is also perfectly reasonable to expect it of a Victorian three-decker novel.

One would not, however, expect the same of a Victorian book in a caoutchouc (unsewn) binding, because these have always disintegrated with the passage of time, and become merely collections of loose leaves inside the publishers case. Book collectors may have fads but they are not fools, and will prefer such books to be restored. Restoration is in fact frequently (and perfectly properly) used to keep a book in usable order. The danger, however—ignoring for the moment the facts that binders skilled in restoration work are not easy to find nor cheap when found—is that by no means all restoration work is or has been undertaken simply in order to keep it in usable shape, and far too seldom do volumes which have been restored bear a note recording the work done. Once a volume has been out of its covers, it is perfectly possible for bookplates to have been switched, leaves washed or substituted, or many other forms of highly questionable doctoring to have been carried out.

Older collectors had a much more swashbuckling attitude than the present generation, and would think nothing of cannibalising two imperfect copies of an Elizabethan play, say, to make up one perfect copy.(16) The existence of sophistication of this sort is accepted as an unavoidable hazard in the acquisition of older material, whereas it would be regarded as a considerable disincentive to purchase more modern material which can be found in undisturbed state.

For books published before the general introduction of publishers cases in the nineteenth century, collectors cannot so easily insist on original bindings. What is sought, rather, is appropriate binding. This really means (ignoring the matter of fine bindings as an unnecessary complication) if not the original bindings in which the volumes were sold by a bookseller then at least one contemporary in style to the date of publication: plain unlettered sheep in the seventeenth century, quarter calf and marbled boards a century later, and so on.

It is in regard to condition, at any rate in so far as it affects the exterior dress of the book, its binding, that it seems to me that the needs of the institutional library and of the private collector diverge strongly. Indeed, the institutional buyer can gain from the exacting requirements of the private purchaser and his insistence on fine condition in the books he adds to his collection. Expressed crudely, the circumstances under which materials are processed, housed and used in an institutional library are such that unless extraordinary pains are taken and there is constant vigilance, its books will be reduced to a state below 'collectors' condition' within a relatively short period. This being the case it is perfectly reasonable to purchase slightly inferior (and considerably cheaper) copies in the first instance.

There are of course some categories of books which belong in special collections to which this consideration does not apply, and which need to be in original bindings and in fine condition for the collection to serve its purposes. In general this will be true of all those collections concerned with the book as an art form and not simply as a vehicle for the text. Collections of fine printing or of private press work are obvious examples, but not the only instances in which this will be true.(17)

Similarly, there are cases in which it will be advantageous if the books are in original bindings, since for many bibliographical purposes examination of bindings, endleaves, advertisement pages and so on may be requisite. However, the fact that such examination is vital in such cases does not mean that scholars *always* need their research material in this form: facsimile editions and microtexts are often used as successfully as if the reader had access to the originals, and in the same way a great many of the needs of users can be met just as well by a rebound volume as by one in its original binding.(18) Rare book librarians, of course, like book collectors are (very reasonably) unusually susceptible to matters of bibliographical importance, but it must not loom too large. Given the opportunity the librarian will prefer a fine to an inferior copy, and go for the certain rather than the disputable, but provided that the binding and other features of a book are not questionable as booksellers' confections many of the library's needs can be met adequately and far more economically by a copy in less than collectors' condition.

Provenance
Pedigrees are useful for books, and to have precise information on a

particular volume's previous whereabouts can often be of value.(19) Obviously it is often not of any particular significance to be able to trace its wanderings before it came into the stock of the dealer from whom it was bought. That a particular book contains the bookplate or signature of, say, Samuel Smiles or E M Forster or Ian Fleming does not in itself make a book more desirable an acquisition for a collection (even though it might influence the dealer's price) unless the collection is particularly concerned with this author, and even then it is of minor interest unless the book is demonstrably one which he used.(20)

Association copies—inscribed by the author to a friend, say—may well command a higher price than usual if either donor or recipient is famous. Equally, books coming from famous collections will normally be more expensive than those of unknown provenance.

Provenance can be particularly important at times. The Parish Library of Loughborough was formed very largely by James Bickham, an eighteenth century rector, but was added to by a number of later incumbents. It is useful to be able to distinguish Bickham's collection from the later accretions by the presence of his bookplate, and instructive to have an inscription in his hand on his copy of the Strawberry Hill Gray's *Odes* saying that it was given him by the author.

The late Harold Nicholson rightly castigated doryphores, the marginal annotators of books. However to have for instance a copy of *Les cinq premiers livres des histoires de Polybe* (Lyons, 1558) bearing annotations in a seventeenth century hand, and to be able to establish through knowledge of the provenance that this was the copy bought by Dryden at the Digby sale in 1680, and that these were his notes which he used in his *Character of Polybius* in 1692—this would be to find treasure-trove indeed.(21) Nicholson's doryphores, in fact, are not always pests.

Institutional libraries are not as a rule very thorough or systematic in attempting to discover and record previous owners of books in their custody, but it is an aspect of rare book librarianship which should not be ignored.

References

1 John Carter, *Taste and technique in book collecting* Cambridge 1948; reprinted with an epilogue Pinner, Private Libraries Association, 1970.

2 Cf Michael Sadleir, *Archdeacon Wrangham* London, Bibliographical Society, 1937; and also Messrs Menno Herzberger's Catalogue no 270, 1973 which lists a baker's dozen of such items, mainly of the nineteenth century.

3 Blackwell's Catalogue no 973 of 1973, includes a good example at item 202: Dunbar's *Poems* collected and edited by David Laing, 2 volumes Edinburgh 1834; one of only two copies printed on vellum.

4 The 'ordinary' edition consisted of 450 copies; there were 50 'specials'.

5 Cf *Chanticleer: a bibliography of the Golden Cockerel Press April 1921—August 1936* London, Golden Cockerel Press, 1936, p 20.

6 Cf John Peters 'Notes on the production of Vine Press books' *Private library* v 7 no 2, Summer 1966, pp 42–4.

7 Cf Pierre Deschamps *Dictionnaire de geographie* Paris, 1870, art. 'Kriech'; Roderick Cave *The private press* London, Faber, 1971, pp 28–9.

8 Statements of limitation, particularly those printed on colophon leaves, are of course notoriously unreliable; the much quoted colophon 'Printed in an edition of one hundred copies, of which this is number two thousand six hundred and eleven' is unkind but worth remembering.

9 Cf L G A Schlichting 'Dutch underground printing' *Print* v 4 no 3 1946, pp 23–8 *and* Anna Simoni 'Dutch clandestine printing 1940–45' *The library* 5th series, v 27 no 1, 1972, pp 1–22.

10 Only 12 copies were printed at the author's private press in 1763. Despite the fact that it was produced in the way which is generally thought most likely to ensure survival, today so far as I am aware there are only three extant copies of the printed text, including that at Dijon.

11 Op cit pp 137–70.

12 G P Winship, in his 'Recollections of a private printer' *The colophon* new series, v 3 no 2, 1938, pp 210–24, recorded how in order to

test the collector's preference for the limited edition, he produced two versions of a particular book; one on hand-made paper at $10, and another much smaller impression on ordinary paper offered at $1.50. The first sold well, the second hardly at all . . .

13 Percy H Muir and John Carter eds *Printing and the mind of man* London, Cassell, 1967.

14 Thomas Marston 'Incunabula and postincunabula' *Library trends* v 9 no 4, April 1961, pp 406–16.

15 Carter however says it better, op cit pp 171–207.

16 Thomas J Wise's plundering of leaves from the British Museum's copies is the most notorious example, but apart from the fact that the leaves were stolen his action was not remarkable by the collecting standards of the time. Cf David Foxon, *Thomas J Wise and the pre-restoration drama* London, Bibliographical Society, 1959.

17 Other instances which spring to mind are natural history illustration, nineteenth century annuals and gift books (of the sort discussed by Anne Renier in *Friendship's offering* London, Private Libraries Association, 1964) and English book illustration of the nineteen-forties (cf Rigby Graham *Romantic book illustration in England 1943–1955* London, Private Libraries Association, 1965).

18 A not untypical example is a study of the Philobiblon Society, the mid-Victorian rival to the Roxburghe Club, on which the present writer was engaged some years ago. For at least nine-tenths of the research involved, use of the rebound volumes of the Philobiblon *Miscellanies* in the British Museum was perfectly satisfactory; it was only for the very minor part of the essay concerned with the physical production of the Society's works that access to copies in the original cloth became necessary.

19 To be able to establish, for example, that the copy of Bartholomew de Chaimis' *Interrogatorium* Mainz, Schoeffer, 1478 (GW6544, Hain *2483, BMC IA 226) now in the Bodleian Library, Pressmark Auct I Q5.15, was the copy which the seventeenth century book collector Richard Smyth 'for the testimony only of the Inscription tending to prove the first Invention of Printing to be at Mentz . . . bestowed on the learned Dr Barlow . . . then Cheife library keeper' as Smyth put it in his manuscript treatise on printing—as can indeed be done

on the basis of a note in Smyth's hand on the colophon leaf of this copy—is useful as a minor note to the history of libraries and of learning in the seventeenth century. Individually insignificant, the accumulation of such information can prove surprisingly useful.

20 Ian Fleming's interest in the novels of Hugh Edwards, for instance, is attested by the introduction he wrote for a new edition of Edwards' *All night at Mr Stanyhurst's* London, Cape, 1963. A copy of one of Edwards' novels coming from Fleming's collection would have more than usual interest.

21 A suppositious example, as the whereabouts of Dryden's copy is not known. Cf T A Birrell 'John Dryden's purchases at two book auctions' *English studies* v 42 no 4, August 1961.

Chapter III
Acquisition of
materials I

Structure of the antiquarian book trade

No trade remains in a state of equilibrium for very long, and the face of antiquarian and second-hand bookselling—of the normal sources of supply for the bulk of materials acquired by a rare books department—has changed very considerably in the past quarter century.

To speak of a single trade is something of an over simplification, and its division into on the one hand stockholding booksellers (large and small, important and insignificant) and on the other those through whose hands stock passes very rapidly, the auction houses, is of considerable age.

The sale of books by auction was introduced into England from the Netherlands in the seventeenth century, the first such sale being that of the library of Lazarus Seaman in November 1676. The method, new to Britain though it had become commonplace in the Netherlands long before this time, proved very successful: over one hundred sales being held in London before the end of the century beside other in the provinces to which the method in turn spread. This way of distributing books did not receive universal approval by any means, both John Evelyn and Samuel Pepys for instance regretted the speed and efficiency with which it permitted collections to be broken up and dispersed. Nevertheless, despite their doubts both were frequenters of auctions and sometimes bought extensively at these sales.(1)

It was not long after the introduction of the method of public auction that specialists in the sale of books by this method appeared. The principal auction houses have a very respectable ancestry—Sotheby, for instance, have been in existence since 1744. When an important collection is to be dispersed, for a considerable period it has been through the agency of one of these specialists; executors and others recognising the considerable pecuniary advantages which accrue from employing their services. A considerable proportion of the more important antiquarian material, in fact, passes through their hands. The method and standard of cataloguing the lots offered for auction is of course variable,(2) the British houses being rather more conservative and less enthusiastic than some other auctioneers in their descriptions of the books for sale. In general, the standard of scholarship in the preparation of the catalogue entries is very high and can be of lasting value, with the result that catalogues of important sales have real importance as works of reference for the trade long after the sale itself, and the record of the prices realised at it, are of no more than historical interest. Runs of these catalogues rightfully command high prices. A subscription to the sale catalogues of the principal auction houses, and to the priced lists of buyers at the sales, is essential for all but the smallest special collections, and the librarian's duties include the pleasant responsibility of scanning these regularly for material of interest which is coming up for sale.

Until relatively recently, a considerable number of books were sold at auctions held by more general auctioneers, in the course of a country house sale for instance. Usually such material was not of the first importance, or at least not recognised as likely to be of significant value by those consigning the books for sale. Such sales, conducted by provincial auctioneers with little knowledge or interest in books were often sad things from the vendor's point of view: the standard of cataloguing was often appalling, the advice given by the auctioneers to the vendors in setting reserve prices sadly deficient, and the publicity given to the sale minimal. When a dealers' 'ring' was also operating, the result was often that the books were sold at prices far lower than they should have fetched or would have realised with more expertise employed on the sellers' behalf.

Books are of course still sold as part of more general sales, and the standard of cataloguing can still be abysmal. But in general far less material appropriate for rare book collections is to be found at such sales as the great increase in book prices (and the publicity given to them) has ensured that valuable material is now more often consigned to a specialist firm to sell. Unless I have been particularly unlucky in the general sales I have attended in recent years, important material is now seldom knocked down at unusually low prices; such is the dearth

35

of antiquarian material for booksellers' stock that they and others bidding at such sales seldom obtain any special bargains. Indeed for bidding (though not from the dealers) to continue past the prevailing market value of the books is commoner at this type of sale than elsewhere. Worth attending for entertainment, they will seldom prove very useful in stock building.

The role of the auction houses in the distribution of rare books is supplemented and indeed surpassed in importance by the specialist antiquarian booksellers. A number of such firms are of distinguished ancestry and have given sterling service to book-collectors and librarians for generations.

The same is true of course of the antiquarian departments of the larger stockholding booksellers. The proportion of old material to new seems to be declining, and certainly the chances of picking up unconsidered trifles from, say, Blackwell's Classical department, or Heffer's natural history stock, are less than they were a few years ago. This is an aspect of the general disappearance of books from the trade over the past few years, which does not affect them alone. The fortunes of such departments wax and wane very much as do those of the large independent booksellers. A good deal of interesting material comes into their stock as part of block purchases of private libraries, though their stock is usually rather less interesting than that of the specialist dealers. Similarly their cataloguing, being less personal and having perforce to range over a greater variety of stock, is often rather below the quality of the best independent firms; but they play a part in the distribution of antiquarian material which is by no means negligible.

Traditionally much of the material which would find its way into the auction rooms or on to the shelves of the fashionable big city booksellers would be found by 'book scouts': men with little or no capital, but with a thorough knowledge of antiquarian books and of the ways of country auctions, the stocks of the junk shops and secondhand dealers on the fringe of the trade. If one may without irreverence misquote Ranganathan, they were men who made or supplemented their livings by procuring for every bookseller his book, for each book its purchaser, and saved the time of the booktrade.

The changing social structure has rendered such men extinct. It should no doubt have caused the individual secondhand bookseller to disappear too, but antiquarian booksellers though by no means economic simpletons are often by nature fierce individualists more concerned with passing a pleasant life than making fat profits. Very frequently some of the most interesting and useful booksellers are men working on their own, or almost so, rather than as a part of a larger organisation. In the nature of things their businesses often cease trading when their owners die or retire, or else change so much in emphasis under new management that they become virtually new firms.(3)

Until relatively recently, for a bookseller to trade successfully, it was vital that he should have premises situated where a sufficient number of his customers could visit him to inspect his stock. The older-established antiquarian dealers are naturally to be found in (or have recently migrated from) the big cities, the university towns, or fashionable spas and watering places. With the very great increases in property rentals, however, allied to a steady increase in institutional rather than personal customers—and in both cases a greater proportion coming from overseas and usually buying through the post rather than by personal visit—as leases have fallen in a greater and greater proportion of important firms have migrated into the country where they encounter lower overheads. Many dealers now—and not only those who have moved into the country—do so much of their business by post that personal visits can be made by appointment only.

In the university towns of course the pattern is rather different, but the overall picture whereby a much greater proportion of antiquarian material is sold by post than was previously the case remains pretty constant.

Another development of relatively recent years is the growth of the part-time or amateur booksellers. There is a long tradition of those who have dealt in books as a sideline, ancillary perhaps to their own book-collecting—and the commerce between booksellers and collectors has always been a two-way one—but it is a modern phenomenon for many specialist dealers to operate strictly as a sideline, working often in a very restricted subject field and with a minuscule stock

37

housed perhaps in a spare bedroom. These dealers represent, one might say, the antiquarian bookworld's version of the boutique, though it is probably more accurate to regard them as the modern equivalent of the departed breed of book scouts.

The scouts were essentially middlemen in the booktrade, however, and the amateurs of today fulfil a different function, serving as an instance of the general trend towards greater specialisation. X will deal only in industrial archaeology; Y sells only books on witchcraft and the occult; Z is interested only in twentieth century poetry. In many cases, since their bookselling is hobby as much as it is business, they are able to assemble very interesting small stocks of books. Some, as they grow larger and more professional, will deal also in new books in their chosen area of subject specialisation. Because of their subject knowledge they can at times produce catalogues which are very useful contributions to bibliographical knowledge in that field, either adding to it or else summarising existing information in a way which for relatively cheap books is uneconomic for the larger and more general firm. Indeed, a good proportion of the stock of these specialists often comes to them from the more general bookshop, just as in the past antiquarian books would migrate to the fashionable bookshop via the quiet country auction and the book scout. And as in that instance, with a mark-up in price which may or may not be reasonable. For these part-time dealers vary considerably in quality, and though the better of them are likely to have a good knowledge of prices in their field and will form a useful source of supply, fewer books pass through their hands than will be the case with professional dealers, and they can get excited about a book of moderate rarity which comes into their stock and set a price on it that will be a lot higher than one would have to pay the cooler-headed professional. And the more amateurish of these spare-time booksellers are just a nuisance.

Another new development in Britain is at the opposite extreme to the amateur, back-bedroom booksellers; a development which stands in relation to traditional antiquarian bookselling rather as Dr Urquhart's methods at the National Lending Library did to conventional library procedures. The methods adopted by Richard Booth at Hay-on-Wye, which have made bookselling the principal industry of the town—to give the obvious example—have caused as many hands to be thrown up in horror and disbelief as was once the case with Boston Spa. But there can be no doubt that these methods have been effectual in changing approaches to the sale of old books, and have enabled many book collectors as well as librarians to profit from them.

It is against this background that the rare books librarian has to formulate his acquisitions policy. The essential questions of *What to buy?*, *from whom?* and *how much?* form part of the substance of this and the succeeding chapter. But before any librarian or book collector can progress far with any of these matters he has to learn the language of the rare book world.

Language of the trade

As with any other specialised group, the language used by those working with rare books takes in many words from related fields (printing, publishing, librarianship or bibliography) and uses them sometimes without change in their meanings, sometimes with subtle changes in emphasis. It takes in many words common in everyday usage, but with a specialised connotation peculiar to the subject. It adds more than a sprinkling of phrases and words which are not used elsewhere, and which are inadequately defined in general dictionaries. Above all, the underlying philosophy and purpose of those concerned with antiquarian books causes a usage as distinctive and peculiar as that of theologians, architects or men in barrack-rooms. Many of the misconceptions about rare books and those concerned with them come from ignorance of this jargon and mistakes as to its meaning.(4)

The standard grammar of bibliophily is of course John Carter's splendid *ABC for book collectors*, now in its fifth edition (London, Hart-Davis, 1968). Armed with this urbane and witty guide—one of the few really readable dictionaries—the novice can embark on the consultation of catalogues and achieve a very reasonable understanding of even the more complex entries they contain. The rare books librarian, in other words, must become (as a critic once described John Carter) 'the kind of man to whom a three-decker means neither a ship of the line nor a sandwich.'

To rely on the *ABC* is not, to be sure, a foolproof method of learning the language, and Mr Carter would be the last to claim his handbook is a comprehensive guide to international usage in the field: it is not, and Carter recommends the use of the polyglot *Dictionary for the antiquarian book-trade* edited by Menno Herzberger for the International League of Antiquarian Booksellers by those who have to read foreign booksellers' catalogues. The cynically minded will also enjoy, as a supplement to Carter, John R Hetherington's 'ABC for booksellers'(5) whose entries like 'AMERICA: The most magical word that you can put in a catalogue. "No copy in America" added to a catalogue entry for eg the LGOC Timetable for Easter 1925 is invaluable' were sufficiently astringent for one antiquarian dealer to resign from the Private Libraries Association in protest when the article was published, although other members of the trade enjoyed it.

The difficulty with the specialised rare book language comes less from the jargon itself than from interpreting the way in which it is applied by individual dealers. To judge precisely how fatigued is a 'tired copy' in the catalogue of dealer A, or at what stage dealer B will cease to describe a book as 'slightly foxed'—or as it will more often be put, 'slightly foxed as usual', implying that nearly all copies will be found in this state—and admit that the book is badly spotted, calls for a considerable knowledge of the standards of those dealers which can be obtained only through experience.

Sources of supply
Knowing from whom one can obtain materials has of course to precede purchase, and the rare books librarian has to build up his own list of the dealers, large and small, specialised or general, highly professional or rather amateurish, as will be appropriate in view of the purchasing interests of his collection. If these interests are solely for material which though hard to obtain is insufficiently in the purview of the antiquarian trade as a whole to figure much in catalogues, he may find that he is served well enough by establishing a good relationship with a local bookseller who will search for the material for him.(6)

For most collections such a passive approach to stock-building is seldom good enough: one has actively to search for the books one requires and get there before other potential purchasers. In establishing his list of dealers likely to have material in the fields in which he is interested the librarian or collector is usually unlikely to be able to limit himself to dealers in only one country. It varies with the subject, language and period of the material being sought, of course: if one is interested only in the history of the steel trade in Sheffield, for instance, one can no doubt afford to ignore continental dealers in a way which would be foolish if one were collecting metallurgical works from Agricola and Biringuccio onwards.(7)

Identification of the large general and specialist dealers who produce catalogues in one's own field of interest is not difficult so far as firms in Britain and North America are concerned. The advertisements in the *Book collector, Papers of the Bibliographical Society of America*, in the back pages of the *Times Literary supplement*, for instance, will provide many useful names and addresses. These sources may be supplemented by a number of specialised guides and directories which are often of particular importance for the smaller dealers whose advertising is limited.

The Sheppard Press produces three such directories: *A directory of dealers in second-hand and antiquarian books in the British Isles*, first published in 1951 with new editions about every four years; *European book dealers* first published in 1967; and *Book dealers in North America*, now in its sixth edition. These convenient and well-arranged volumes between them cover the more important dealers in most parts of the world fairly well; their principal disadvantage is that delays between collection of material for new editions and their eventual publication makes much of the information they contain out of date soon after publication, and the delay between editions aggravates the problem.

For booksellers in Britain the Sheppard Press directory is supplemented by Gerald Coe's *The complete booksellers directory* (Wilbarston, Market Harborough, Gerald Coe, 1969) a successor to the same editor/compiler's *Small booksellers and collectors directory* (1967) which as the title implies concentrated on those smaller dealers about whom it is so often difficult to find information. Less convenient in format than the Sheppard guides, Coe has the great advantage of including many of the smaller part-time dealers; being produced very

41

soon after collection of the information it is consequently less often out of date as regards changes of address and the like. Its major drawback also derives from the method of compilation: being based entirely on questionnaires completed by the booksellers, with no entries for those who failed to return them, there are some very remarkable omissions of some of the largest and most important antiquarian dealers.

A third directory listing dealers in Britain is the *Annual directory of booksellers specialising in antiquarian and out of print books* issued by the publishers of the specialist trade paper *The clique* and first published in 1969. Though also useful, it is less full than either Sheppard or Coe.(8)

Another directory sometimes useful, and with the advantage of covering the whole world in a single volume, is B Donald Grose, *The antiquarian booktrade, an international directory of subject specialists*, Metuchen NJ, Scarecrow Press, 1972. The volume claims to list almost two thousand dealers throughout the world, arranging them first under headings of their subject specialisation and then in an alphabetical sequence giving the full name and address. No indication of size of stock, hours of opening or other information is given, and the omission of many full-time dealers of importance (and nearly all the part-timers) limit its value very considerably.

In addition to these guides, the International League of Antiquarian Booksellers from time to time produces a directory listing all the bookseller members of the Antiquarian Booksellers' Association, the Antiquarian Booksellers' Association of America, and the various other national groups affiliated to the ILAB.(9) Though by no means without its uses, the ILAB directory suffers the usual drawbacks of multinational publications and is in the nature of things limited to the larger firms.

Like so many trade directories, these various guides are all more or less inadequate when it comes to the subject indexes which are obviously of great importance to the librarian or book collector trying to trace those who deal in his particular field of interest. If in one directory some booksellers are listed as specialising in 'Nineteenth century literature' and others as dealers in 'Literature (19th and 20th centuries)' one may with reason curse the compilers for inconsistency, but one still has a pretty good idea that both groups are going to be of use if one is developing a collection of, let us say, the work of Mrs Gaskell. But are those other booksellers included under the headings 'Literature' or 'Old and rare literature' or those strangely unwordly people who claim to specialise in 'Books and prints' likely to be worth contacting? One has no idea.

As a result of these deficiencies in recording booksellers' areas of subject specialisation it is often necessary to supplement the directories' information in other ways. Leaving on one side for the moment the reading of catalogues and personal inspection of their stock, it is often possible to gather a good deal about a firm's approach and range of interests from its advertisements (for books wanted as well as offered for sale) in the trade journals such as *AB bookman's weekly* and *The clique*. Similarly, one's examination of auction catalogues against the lists of prices and buyers, can be very useful although the dealer may of course have been acting as agent for a client and not just buying for his own stock. Finally notes on recent catalogues, of the sort included in the *Book collector*, and the lists of catalogues recently received which appear in the *American book collector* can often provide a lead to booksellers with material potentially of interest.

Having established a list of probable sources of supply, the next step is to make contact with the dealers. To pay personal visits is obviously the ideal method, and most antiquarian bookmen (whether librarian or collector) will take such opportunities whenever they occur. Quite apart from the chance of inspecting the dealer's stock, it is both enjoyable and instructive to know the man with whom one will be dealing. One can gauge his approach and standards far more rapidly through even a brief conversation and cursory inspection of his books than any other way.

When the bookseller is pursuing his trade full-time and has a shop, such contacts can be made very easily and with little formality. With the part-time dealers, and those others whose stock can be inspected by appointment only, one naturally feels a little diffident about making a special visit when as so often it turns out that there is nothing either currently or potentially in that dealer's stock which one would wish to purchase. But it is worth remembering that the booksellers are also anxious to extend their contacts with possible customers, and that they will accept that these appointments may be no more fruitful than other blind dates.

In many cases it is of course impracticable to establish personal contact in this way, although personal visits are always desirable. Antiquarian bookmen's tales tend to be rather like those of fishermen in improving with time (though usually more concerned with books caught than those which got away), but too many of them are concerned with the books found in unexpected places—whether while killing time waiting for a train in Swansea, or getting lost in the back streets of Brussels, or arriving in Farringdon Road at the same time as new stock on the book barrows, or wherever does not matter—for the librarian to neglect such chances, however unpromising the shop or stall may seem. If he is a real bookman he will need no prompting.

Contacts made by post are inevitably less satisfactory, although with the passage of time the relationship may be transformed completely.(10) The easiest course is simply to write to be put on the dealer's mailing list for catalogues. To do this may be sufficient, but it is worthwhile taking rather more trouble and indicating the areas in which one is collecting (and with a lot more precision than the dealers' interests are recorded in the trade directories!).

The interests of the antiquarian bookseller and of the rare books librarian are after all closely allied, and booksellers take a good deal of interest and indeed pride in helping to build up the collections of their clients. But they can take this personal interest only if in the confidence of the collector or librarian, and a simple request for catalogues followed from time to time by orders for specific items in these is scarcely sufficient. Just as the personal visit to a bookshop will enable one to inspect stock not yet and perhaps never to be catalogued, so when one has built up the right relationship with a dealer by post one will often be offered the chance to buy material in advance of its being listed in a catalogue.

Equally important, when as often happens the dealer receives two or three orders for the same book by the same post, he will prefer to sell it to the customer to whom he knows its acquisition is valuable.

And there are times also when books are offered for sale which are badly needed for the collection in one's care, yet which for budgetary reasons cannot at once be ordered or paid for. The establishment of a personal relationship with booksellers makes all these things easier for the rare books librarian. It is obviously simpler with the small firm than the large, but even in the larger firms one is normally dealing with human beings and not computers, and few antiquarian booksellers are so large that personal contacts can't be made.

Collectors and librarians are sometimes chary about revealing the scope and nature of their buying interests to the booktrade, apparently in the belief that by doing so they will enable the dealers to mark up the prices of books which they are seeking to a higher level than they would otherwise be asked to pay. That there are booksellers who will do this I have no doubt, but few librarians have such a long purse and short time in which to buy as to make it worthwhile. If the librarian suspects he is being taken for a sucker the remedy is in his own hands in any case. But such instances are so uncommon that they are scarcely worth taking into account in formulating one's general policy, which will be better served by regarding the bookseller as ally rather than antagonist.

Prices
The question of how much to pay is one which must exercise the mind of the rare books librarian in many different ways. It is obviously of significance in deciding one's acquisition policy in the first place, since the prevailing prices for some material will place it beyond reach. When hoping to buy at an auction, one needs to know the book's value and have some idea of the price it is likely to realise (which may very well be considerably different) in order to establish the limit to which one is prepared to go before dropping out of the bidding. If offered material by booksellers, one has to weigh the asking price against the fair market valuation and one's need for the book in one's library.

Knowledge of current market prices, which may be very different from the prices which have been paid for books already in the library, is also important for insurance purposes; as indeed it serves also as a rough and ready guide to the need to remove books from a library's open shelves into the greater security of special collections.

A certain degree of this knowledge of prices will be carried in the librarian's mind. If one has been checking auctioneer's and booksellers' catalogues for some time one will have an approximate notion of prevailing prices for some of the more frequently occurring books in one's field of interest. To compile one's own price index for such material is not difficult, and is well worth the effort involved.(11)

The drawback is that a good deal of the material one seeks is not likely to be offered for sale so frequently as to figure in one's own index more than once or twice if at all. One has therefore to supplement this personal index of values by reference to other tools of the trade. The auction houses themselves will on request furnish estimates of the price they expect particular books to realise in a forthcoming sale. This can serve as a substitute for further research on one's own account, but their estimates are understandably rather conservative and should be regarded as being of the 'not less than X' kind. Though useful, such estimates will probably form only a small proportion of the total one needs.

Of the various guides, the most useful are *American book prices current*, which has been appearing annually since 1895, and *Book auction records*, which is also an annual and was first published in 1901. Both include details of all except the cheapest books sold at the principal auction houses. *ABPC* is not (as its title suggests) limited to American sales, having covered the London auction houses since 1958, and is in many respects superior to its British rival: John Carter aptly describes *BAR* as 'compiled rather than edited'; a criticism which cannot be levelled at *ABPC*. Delays in the production of the annual volumes have at times been rather too long, but a run of one or other (and often both) forms one of the most-consulted of booksellers' reference books. In the past there was a third such work, *Book prices current* which appeared annually from 1887 to 1948 and twice afterwards at four year intervals. Better edited and rather fuller in its detail than *BAR*, the information its volumes contain is now of course of little value for ascertaining current prices.

Much newer than these three (and therefore still much less useful) is *Bookman's price index*, edited by Daniel McGrath for the Gale Research Company since 1964. Whereas the other guides are essentially cumulations of auction catalogues, *BPI* is a cumulation of the catalogues of selected booksellers for a given period, arranged in alphabetical author sequence. A defect of the guide is that it represents only a small proportion of the antiquarian books in the Anglo-American market in the period covered by each volume, as it includes so few catalogues from specialist dealers. Some books sold at auction later figure in dealers' catalogues of course, and many of these will therefore be recorded in *BPI* (and very usefully at the bookseller's price) but for those books auctioned which do not subsequently appear in a bookseller's list *ABPC* or *BAR* remain the only easy source of information on prices.

From consultation of a few years' issues of these various guides it is possible to ascertain that copies of a certain book have realised such and such prices in the past. But such easily found information is deceptive, since the information about the copies given in each of the guides is necessarily very brief. So brief does it have to be in fact that it may well omit some detail on condition which led to the setting of the price at that level.

To find from consultation of these guides that (say) a copy of the Kelmscott *Chaucer* was sold at Sotheby's in 1968 for £850, another by Parke-Bernet in New York the same year for $2000, and that a specialist dealer was offering a third copy in 1970 for $1875, without also finding out that the first was from the library of Sir Sydney Cockerell (and therefore of important provenance) that the second was in a binding by T J Cobden-Sanderson, and the third accompanied by a number of trial proofs of the engravings—in short, that all three possessed feature likely to improve their market standing—is not very helpful when in 1976 one is trying to gauge whether the price being asked for a very ordinary copy is a fair one.

Similarly, for material which appears only very rarely on the market a record of the prices previously realised is often of very little help. To know that X was sold for twenty guineas at the Hartletop sale in 1907, that another was bought-in at $140 in New York in 1932 and that the book has not subsequently appeared in the auction rooms, is precious little use unless one knows also whether the Hartle-top auction was a 'celebrity' sale,(12) whether the New York market was depressed in 1932, what the pound/dollar exchange rate was at the time, what the general progression of prices in this subject field has been,(13) and so on. To the experienced man with his finger on the pulse of the antiquarian booktrade the information which can be gleaned from these guides can be very useful and indicative; to the novice it can be dangerous.

Very often the question resolves itself much more simply than the above paragraphs may suggest. One learns to recognise that some dealers habitually set higher prices on their stock than others, and therefore to regard all their prices with a more cautious eye than those of more conservative firms. If the book is sufficiently common, one may hope to be able to buy it at a price set by the latter rather than the former.

In many instances too close attention to buying at the lowest possible price is undesirable. Needing rather urgently examples of the books illustrated by the nineteenth century process called 'nature printing' some years ago, approaches were made to specialist dealers in natural history and in typography—as so often happens the books in question fell into two distinct areas of specialisation—to try to obtain them. A natural history dealer quoted £16 for a recased copy of one of these books; a dealer in typography offered another copy of the same book in a not unpleasing contemporary morocco binding for £22. Very similar prices considering the difference in condition between the sets, and both reasonable as regards our estimate of the prevailing market value. As the cheaper copy was adequate for our purpose that was bought. It was tiresome some time later to find a third copy in a miscellaneous list from a general dealer priced at £7, which was considerably below its market value.(14) Very possibly we would have found this copy had already been sold had we then attempted to buy it; and as I have not since seen any copies priced at less than £30 I have no doubt that our decision to purchase the copy we did was correct.

In periods in which money is declining rapidly in value, as at the present, expertise in calculating 'correct' market prices is perhaps to be discounted. For the risk facing the librarian who pays too close attention to prices is similar to that of the military strategist, to whom the danger of trying to refight the last war with the last war's weapons is an occupational hazard. A knowledge of last year's prices is an excellent thing, but it is this year's price one will be asked to pay. In *Taste and technique in book collecting* John Carter enumerated ten rules around the matter of prices,(15) of which the last is the most important: 'Be less afraid of paying a stiff price than of letting slip some book you know to be rare and which is important to you. You cannot tell when, at what price, or even whether, you will see another.'

Purchasing of antiquarian material

During his routine checking of catalogues from the auction houses the rare books librarian will from time to time come across lots containing books he is seeking for his collection and which, he believes from his own experience and such information as he has been able to cull from the auction price guides, are likely to be sold at prices his institution can pay. How is he to set about buying them for his library?

It is sometimes possible for a librarian to attend at an auction sale in person; if as is more often the case this cannot be managed, it is always possible to place a bid with the auctioneer by post. Possible for the private collector at any rate, but for the librarian wishing to buy on behalf of his institution the auction room is often fraught with problems. Finance officers often regard the idea of buying material at a price unfixed until the transaction takes place as being highly improper if not in fact likely to undermine the whole basis of society; they want nothing to do with it.

Permission to place bids, then, is seldom forthcoming. But quite apart from this difficulty, which could be resolved were it really necessary, it is hardly ever desirable to buy directly at auctions. Quite apart from the matter of bidding technique (and the risk that one will get the bit between one's teeth, especially after several lots in which one was interested have been knocked down to others) it is worth considering carefully the conditions of sale printed in the auction catalogues. These amount to an almost complete disclaimer of any warranty in respect of the books offered for sale; it is very much a

49

matter of *caveat emptor*.

If instead of placing bids directly, the rare books librarian commissions a bookseller to bid on his behalf—the normal practice, in fact—he gains a lot more than just a bidding agent. He will have the benefit of the bookseller's advice on the worth of the book and the price it is likely to realise, and of his professional skill in examining and collating it before the sale; in other words of obtaining all the protection normally afforded those buying from a reputable bookseller.(16) Furthermore the librarian will be buying the book in the way understood by and acceptable to his finance officers. For these extra advantages the extra price that he has to pay, ten per cent of the price at auction (that is of successful commissions) is by no means unreasonable.

With auction sales, there is sufficient time between initial receipt of the catalogue and the date of the sale for consideration and consultation. With booksellers' catalogues however the position is very different, and time is of the essence. Catalogues need to be examined as soon as received, and decisions on whether to order or not be made without any delay.

How necessary this is may be illustrated by the fact that on more than one occasion I have received a catalogue in the morning's post, telephoned the bookseller with an order before ten o'clock and still been told that the books I required had already been sold that same morning; in some cases several orders having preceded mine. And these were by no means under-priced books being snapped up by bargain hunters.

The need for this sort of urgency, which is very real indeed as far as the more sought-after books are concerned although some proportion of the books offered in a catalogue may remain unsold for some time, makes nonsense of the normal rather leisurely acquisition procedures of libraries. The traditional methods, whereby an acquisitions librarian in a university library will send a new catalogue to a member of the academic staff for any suggestion he may make for purchase and when these are received check them against the library's holdings before preparing the order—a method which usually takes weeks rather than hours—will still turn up some books but hardly many unless they are priced at more than the prevailing market rate. The routines must be gone through, of course, with official orders being prepared and so on, but these should be in the nature of confirmation of orders placed by telephone or cable. Antiquarian booksellers do not go to the trouble of putting a codeword in their catalogues(17) for their own amusement, but to make ordering easier for their more distant customers. And telephoned orders from California to London are by no means unheard of. . . .

In order to gain time for manoeuvre and to steal a march over their competitors, rare book librarians will often seek ways to have catalogues sent to them in advance of the general mailing. It is commonplace for libraries in the United States, for example, to pay to have catalogues sent them by airmail. Some will go as far as requesting proofs of the catalogues to be sent them in this way. Many booksellers will reasonably enough oblige good customers by seeing that they receive catalogues earlier than the common herd. Others will endeavour so to dispatch their catalogues that all on the regular mailing list receive them at about the same time.(18) In either case the game is to the swift, and it is the librarian's duty to get the catalogues as soon as possible, make his selections and place his orders with the minimum of delay.

References

1 John Lawler *Book auctions in England in the seventeenth century* London, Elliot Stock, 1898 is the standard though now badly dated work; offset litho reprint by Gale Research Co, 1968.

2 Important books are usually described very fully, and run-of-the-mill material more briefly; minor material may be totally concealed in entries which list one or two books briefly and then add 'and six more' or some other omnium gatherum phrase.

3 Percy Muir *Minding my own business* London, Chatto & Windus, 1956, and his 'Further reminiscences' included from time to time in the *Book collector*, and Richard Brown and Stanley Brett *The London bookshop* Pinner, Private Libraries Association, v 1 1971, v 2 1974, give an excellent idea of such changes in the trade.

4 The popular confusion as to the meaning of 'uncut copy', for

instance.

5 In *Private library* vol 8 no 2, Summer 1967, pp 43–6.

6 The present writer has found this method perfectly satisfactory in trying to collect early war-time issues of 'Puffin picture books' for example. In the case of much locally printed or published material, eg the chapbooks produced in Onitsha before the Nigerian civil war, employment of a local buying agent on the American pattern is probably the only way to get good results.

7 Localised rarity has already been discussed in Chapter I. It would no doubt be possible to formulate a rule on the location of antiquarian material which I suspect would prove not unlike Bradford's law of scattering.

8 A very useful comparative review of the three can be found in *Private library* 2nd series, vol 3 no 3, Autumn 1970, pp 162–4.

9 Lists of members of the different member associations can be obtained from the associations themselves.

10 Cf Helene Hanff *84 Charing Cross Road* London, Deutsch, 1971.

11 An author/short title record on cards, bearing such annotations as 'Sotheby 16 June '68 lot 349 £28; Hogg cat 92 '71 no 67 £35; Dawsons cat 54 '72 $85' performs very well, and provided one has (as one should) kept a file of the catalogues it is very easy to refer back to them for fuller information. Some librarians prefer a file of cuttings from the catalogues thus obviating the need to refer back, but as this destroys the catalogues for all other purposes it is not to be recommended.

12 In other words one at which the fame of the collector or library being sold makes for higher prices, even for minor items, than at miscellaneous sales. The classic instance is the celebrated Roxburghe sale of 1812. Market prices tend to rise to the level set at celebrity sales, but this does not always happen rapidly.

13 The Times/Sotheby price indexes can be of some use here, but call for shrewd handling. John Carter is not alone in preferring Nicolas Barker's splendid 'The aesthetic investor's guide to current literary values, an essay in bibliometry' in *Book collector* vol 9 no 4, Winter 1960, pp 414–22.

14 'Bargains may be obtained off the counters of the most acute' as W C Hazlitt observed in his *The book collector* London, 1904, p 94. My

own favourite instance is of a Loughborough library school student who, visiting an antiquarian bookseller to sell a copy of Churchill's *Savrola* walked out having bought a book from the dealer's half-crown shelf for an inferior edition of which Quaritch were asking £28. Cf Philip West 'A quest for *The toilet*' in *Private library* vol 7 no 1, Spring 1966, pp 13–5. But it would be absurd to let the hope of such bargains influence one's purchasing policy.

15 John Carter, *Taste and technique* . . . pp 134–6, in the course of his Chapter X, 'Bookshop and auction room' which is really obligatory reading for all concerned in the sale of antiquarian books.

16 Dealers can exceed their commissions and purchase at prices above the limits set by their clients, but it will be at their own risk as the famous Dr Rosenbach discovered when he did so once too often. The notorious case of the 'only known copy' of *Tom Jones*, 1749, in original boards (which proved to have twelve leaves supplied from the second edition) in which Lord Rothschild successfully entered a suit for recovery of the purchase price, is a good instance of the protection buyers have against booksellers' errors of judgement. Cf Edwin Wolfe 2nd and John Fleming *Rosenbach, a biography* London, Weidenfeld & Nicolson, 1961.

17 eg 'The codeword for this catalogue is CASLON, meaning "Please send from your catalogue no 87 the following items".'

18 'To offset the delays in Transatlantic (and other) mails, no copies of this catalogue will be dispatched in Great Britain or Europe until delivery has taken place in North America.' Keith Hogg, Catalogue no 98.

Chapter IV
Acquisition of materials II

As was suggested in Chapter III, the librarian in charge of a special collection is not often going to be in the position that he can simply sit back and wait for his stock to come to him, whether from bookshop or auction room. A collection *can* be built up in this haphazard way provided time is not of importance and the material is not also being sought by other libraries or collectors, but a purposeful and coherent acquisitions policy will demand that other methods also be employed.

At the core of this policy must lie the desiderata list, the record of those books which the institution knows it needs for the systematic development of the collection. The list will be built up in a number of ways, of which the principal will be the examination of the present collection by the rare books librarian and others expert in the subject field,(1)in the light of the general policy for its growth, to reveal those key books and editions—and also the secondary material—which are not yet in its stock, and are necessary to round it out. The specialised knowledge of the personnel will of course be supplemented by the use of the appropriate specialist bibliographies which will add further to the list.

Research libraries are as a rule very glad to receive suggestions for books which should be added from readers using the collections, as in the nature of things the directions in which research may proceed will not always be apparent. Not all suggestions will be taken up, since some will be in conflict with general policy for the library's development, but the others form an important second category of material which one will seek to purchase. A third group of additions to a library's list of desiderata will come from those books it has sought unsuccessfully to buy at auction sales or from booksellers' catalogues.

The list of books wanted for a special collection will not include only details of author, title and so forth(2) plus such information on market value or auction prices realised as might be obtainable. These are all necessary, but the list will also need to include an indication of the books' importance in the growth of the collection if it is really to be of use.

One cannot automatically transfer details of books unsuccessfully ordered to the desiderata list, because in some cases they may, for example, have been orders for material of secondary importance which were placed because that copy was being offered at an unusually advantageous price, or because (being scarce) the seeming opportunity to purchase it could not be neglected. One needs therefore to have a record of what is vital for the collection and must be obtained without overmuch regard for the price, of what is very desirable if the price is right, and of what would be useful if funds were more abundant than usual—as for instance towards the end of a financial year when unspent money will be lost.

From their own index of desiderata in these various categories it is normal practice for libraries to prepare lists which they will send to an appropriate dealer to search for on their behalf. The advantages of close relationships with the antiquarian booksellers, already alluded to in the previous chapter, will be readily apparent. The dealer, having received the list, after checking it against his own stock will search in the antiquarian trade for the books it includes, by means of advertisements in the appropriate journals like *The clique* and *AB bookman's weekly*. If one is fortunate, other dealers will send him quotations for some of the books on the list, which he will then transmit to the library.

Dealers normally perform this service with no charge to the library beyond their mark-up on the books which are actually supplied, and will continue to search for those items they have not been able to supply for a considerable time.(3) The process is obviously one of diminishing returns, though, and one cannot expect a great flow of material which has been sought by advertisements over a long period.

In preparing desiderata lists for submission to the trade there are a number of rules one has to observe. By sending a dealer a list of desiderata one is entering into a moral contract with him to buy those books for which he can furnish quotations which are reasonably in line with the prevailing market price. If one declines to purchase a book for which a dealer has advertised *at his own expense* because one has set on it a value to one's library which is lower than the asking price, and the dealer was not informed of the limitation, or (to give another example) one declines an offered copy which is in full morocco because one wants it only in original boards and this was not stipulated in the desiderata list—then one is not going to find that dealer taking too much trouble searching for one's desiderata in the future.

To send too extensive a list at one time is unwise, since one can scarcely expect as diligent and intensive searching for several hundred books as one can for a score or two. (The lists sent to the trade will therefore form only a selection of those items included in the working file of desiderata for internal use). If the list is very extensive, should the dealer be able to turn up a substantial number it may well create problems with one's bookfund. The lists need to be modest in extent and explicit about such matters as what will be regarded as acceptable condition. It may be felt dangerous to include on them the price one is prepared to pay, but a good dealer will not take advantage of it, since one's continuing custom will be worth more to him than a quick profit. The advantage is that the dealer will advise one if the limits set are unrealistic in terms of prevailing prices.

Sometimes libraries will supply the same desiderata list to a number of different booksellers, in the hope that by spreading their enquiries they will end up with more offers than by working through a single dealer. This is not often likely to be the case if the dealer one selects as single agent is competent; and has a number of disadvantages. If several advertisements for the same book appear in the trade papers the suggestion that the book is widely in demand may well drive up the price. In addition, the individual dealer is likely to search less assiduously than if he has the sole agency.(4)

At times it may be felt advantageous to bypass the trade, and to advertise directly for books wanted, as some libraries do in *The spectator*, for instance. Such advertising, because it taps other potential sources of supply, can occasionally be useful, but in general the returns are much slighter than those obtained by working through the bookseller agent.

Gifts

Although the purchase of material forms the most consistent means of enlarging the stock of special collections, in many respects it is of less importance than the acquisition of material by gift, as a glance at the history of any large research collection will show.

Gifts may be of many kinds. As well as the presentation of books in their owner's lifetime, or by his bequest, there may be the presentation of money to augment the library's bookfund for the purchase of books in a specific subject area (or even for the purchase of a particular book). There is the concealed gift, in which the library is given the opportunity to buy a complete collection, or its choice of books from it, at a price considerably lower than the owner knows he could obtain on the open market. Or the virtual gift, when owners without surrendering legal ownership of material will deposit it in a library and make it generally available for scholarly consultation—the deposit of many private archives in record offices is a good instance of the way in which owners of material have been relieved of the everyday cares of custodianship, and valuable records preserved for posterity. In the long term such deposited material will frequently become the property of the library housing it.(5) At times material will be presented to a library as a quid pro quo for services rendered by the library. Occasionally a munificent donor will present not just books or financial assistance but will create an entirely new library, although because of the different tax structure in recent years this has been very much more rare in Britain than in North America.

The processes of soliciting and organising a flow of gifts are far less amenable to the development of a systematic method than are those of acquisition by purchase. The strategy and tactics to be employed have to be varied for the particular case.

'Take what you want' said God. 'Take it, and pay for it.' The proverb is apposite in the case of gifts to libraries: one may take, but the fact that one does not pay cash should not conceal the truth that one has to pay in some other way instead. Just as one does not blithely purchase books without regard for the market price and the other factors already discussed, so one has to consider whether gifts are worth the price one has to pay.

With the outright offer of individual books for the collection the matter is a simple one, and the price is usually no more than than the appropriate expression of thanks to the donor.(6) When more than the presentation of an individual volume is concerned, and in some instances even then, there are other factors to be taken into account before the gift is accepted.

It is helpful to consider why people offer gifts to libraries in order to appreciate some of the factors which operate. Visiting an exhibition of (let us say) books put out by mission presses, and talking to one of the library staff, I remember that I have in my attic a trunk full of the gospels in Tibetan, Gujerati and other languages with which a great-uncle sowed the seed many years ago. The collection has enough sentimental value to prevent me throwing them in the dustbin, but not too much as I cannot read the books. Fired by the exhibition, I realise that the books might well enrich their collections, and offer them as a gift. As another instance, the grieving widow of a bank manager with a taste for the Georgian poets, recollecting the affection with which he used to speak of his old school, decides to present his collection to the school library as a memorial to him, and wishes it to be kept as a collection distinct from the rest of the library. As a third case, when a retired professor of history dies, he bequeaths to his old university his personal library (rich in material dealing with the Franco-Prussian war and its aftermath) plus the substantial but ill-organised mass of his own working papers, which may have some value for other scholars working in the same field. For a fourth example, a book collector who professes himself interested in one of the new universities, intimates to the librarian that he would be willing to present a couple of minor incunables to its library.

These four imaginary examples illustrate some of the problems which the library must face. In the first instance, though I profess to be offering my great-uncle's books with no strings attached, before the librarian can accept my gift (which may, for all either of us know contain some very useful accessions to the library's research collections, or be all rubbish) he must ensure that I have no unvoiced reservations about his use of the material. Am I willing for them to add those books which will be useful, and to dispose of the others as they think fit? If they do not want everything, do I want the discards returned to me? Am I prepared to give the books to the library for the staff to work through at leisure, or do I want them to come to make the selection at my home?

In the second case, considerable tact is clearly needed. There is, on the one hand, the human duty to give sympathy, and in such cases it can relieve the sense of loss for mourners if they can feel that there will be an appropriate and tangible memorial. The call of common humanity can easily be in conflict with professional considerations. A closed collection of the sort indicated is not likely to be of much benefit to the school. Furthermore a school library is not, perhaps, the best home for such a collection if it is to be a living memorial and not just a dead collection locked in a case and never used—often the fate of such donations, but hardly what is intended by those giving them.

With the books and research papers on the Franco-Prussian war, other considerations apply. Is the subject one still of interest to the university? Has the library the financial resources to continue to augment the collection, so that it remains live and useful? Has it the space to house it? Has it the human resources to sort and calendar the professor's papers so that they will be accessible to scholars? Benefactions impose obligations for the host library, as Bodley's librarian observed in his evidence to the Parry Committee, (7) and in more than a few instances libraries have felt obliged to refuse collections because they lacked the resources to continue to develop them.

The fourth case presents fresh problems. No new university is likely to embark on the collection of fifteenth century books so the proffered gift will not fit in with the institution's acquisition policies. The books will impose problems of custodianship, and be virtually unused museum pieces, whereas in a library already rich in incunabula they might prove a very useful adjunct to the collection.(8) However, the offer was made from the best motives, and to refuse outright (however tactfully) might be to destroy the possibility of future benefactions not only from the same source but also from others.(9)

Dealing with gifts, as with the operation of the library service as a whole, is not simply the application of some tenets and rules, it is a matter of *style*. There are some libraries in which the user feels the staff to be actively interested in serving him and to go beyond the simple call of duty in doing so, just as with others equally well stocked and equipped one gets the impression that no more than minimal service will be given. It is no accident that those libraries which benefit considerably from donations are those in which the staff have this gift of showing their interest in the collections under their care and in the research activities of their clients.

Some of the work undertaken by rare book librarians (in publications, exhibitions and so forth, and extramurally in the activities of bibliographical and other societies), which are dealt with in other chapters, will be influential in encouraging donations. To some extent these duties should be regarded as the price to be paid for gifts, although obviously they will have to be undertaken as part of the department's normal responsibilities.

In other respects, the way in which the rare book librarian will set about soliciting gifts will be many and varied. He will not, of course, be so cold-blooded and meanly calculating as this chapter may suggest. As a bookman and scholar he will naturally keep in contact not only with professional colleagues but with private collectors and amateurs in the same field.(10) He will naturally devote much of his time to showing the collections in his care to interested visitors, and to giving them hospitality. He will naturally take considerable pains in dealing with postal enquiries.(11) In these and in similar ways he will show the users of his collections that his library is actively and enthusiastically devoted to the advancement of knowledge. The costs of such activities are high in staff time, but so are the returns in staff satisfaction—and in the ways in which users, in turn, will try to repay some of the services they have received.

To be good at attracting donations to his library, the rare books librarian must then combine the erudition of the scholar, the enthusiasm of the lover and the persuasiveness of the con-man. An eminent American librarian has suggested, not altogether frivolously, that these qualities are not all that is needed: that today only men with private means can be successful rare book librarians, as only they can afford to belong to the right clubs, lunch their prospective victims at the right restaurants, meet them at the right parties . . .

Non-rare materials
As well as the rare books which are the main concern of a special collection, there are other categories of material which properly belong with such a collection:

i *Facsimile editions*, modern reproductions of books appropriate in the collection. A library will naturally and correctly prefer to purchase original editions if they can be obtained and if the library has the financial resources, since only the original editions will be satisfactory for all types of research. However, since in practice neither original copies nor funds are available in the quantities needed it is good sense for the library to obtain facsimile editions instead when these are available. The passive approach is to buy offset litho reprints, such as the excellent and reasonably priced series put out by the Scolar Press. The active approach is also to obtain copies (in microtext or full size electrostatic copy) of those books which otherwise could not be obtained at all. The Institute of Jamaica, for instance, which has been collecting West Indiana assiduously for over half a century is very considerably enriched as a working collection by the presence in it of copies made from the unique originals in the Archivo de Indias at Seville, the Public Records Office and elsewhere. Not all the needs of users in Jamaica are met by such copies, but infinitely more than if the enquirers had to go to Seville or London to see these texts.

The advantage of facsimile editions and of other copies is not limited to the relatively cheap provision of materials which would otherwise be absent from the collection. The wear and tear on fragile material in the library can also be reduced, by providing readers with copies in place of the original in those cases that the copy will serve their needs. Most readers will find the 'feel' of a modern offset litho reprint easier than the original, and the risks inherent in its use are much less.

To be sure, there are difficulties in the use of facsimile editions. Not all reprinting agencies are punctilious in stating the source of their text: a matter which may be of particular importance especially in

61

textual studies. Not all employ editors of sufficient bibliographical expertise to ensure that the reprinted text reproduces its original in a satisfactory way: that whatever retouching is technically necessary is without bibliographical significance. Not all reproduce the work in the same size as the original, or are explicit about the changes made in the size of the reproduction. Not all, having appointed an editor of recognised standing in that particular field, allow him the degree of control over the production that scholarship demands. Very few allow the editor to provide a substantial introduction or other ancillary matter which will enrich the usefulness of the facsimile edition for the research student.

There are examples of modern facsimiles which are models of what such work should be. To take examples from my own collection, good instances are the Printing Historical Society's facsimiles of Charles Manby Smith's *The working man's way in the world* (1853) with preface and notes by Ellic Howe, and Vincent Figgins' *Type specimens* (1801 and 1815) edited by Berthold Wolpe. Because of the excellence of the editing, both these will normally be preferred to the originals by most typography students. Their very modest price, compared with many other reprints, shows that it is perfectly feasible to produce such edited reprints at reasonable cost. Another usefully edited reprint is the *Type specimen of the Vatican Press* (1628) edited by H D L Vervliet, and others in the same series published by Herzberger/VanGendt in Amsterdam. Some of the other commercial reprinting houses eg Scolar Press are of similar high standard.

Even with those reprints which are less satisfactory, however, it is usually a matter of bewailing lost opportunities for good work. I may with some justice complain that the quality of printing in my reprint of James Watson's *History of printing* (1713) is murkier than it should be; or that because my reprint of M D Fertel's *La science pratique de l'imprimerie* (1723) is simply described by the publishers as 'slightly reduced from the original' I cannot use it as well as if it were original size or I knew the scale of reduction—but I much prefer these to the alternative of having no copies at all.

ii *Microtexts* may at times be the only way of obtaining copies of rare materials which are needed for the collection. In some instances other microforms may be acquired, but in most of the cases that a library has to order copies of rare material from the libraries holding it either positive or negative microfilm will normally be supplied. Negative microfilm will be cheaper, but has some disadvantages.(12) Whether positive or negative be obtained, it is vital that the degree of reduction be known (at least by the presence of a scale on it). The special equipment needed to house the film and make it usable present housekeeping problems for the librarian; it is very desirable that among this equipment should be a reader capable of variable enlargement since some types of research make it vital that the user should be able to work from an image the same size as the original.

iii *Electrostatic reprints* and other full-size copies will usually be preferred to microtexts by the users of the library. Since certain types of material can scarcely be used in microtext—library catalogues, for instance—it is necessary to obtain full-size copies whenever the characteristics of the material and its potential use justify the extra cost. Frequently, of course, since many libraries very properly forbid the making of electrostatic copies directly from their rare books, it will be necessary to have a microfilm made as an intermediate step.

As with microtexts, it is vital that the size of the original be indicated on the copy. By no means all electrostatic copiers produce copies exactly the same size as the original, although at a cursory inspection they may appear the same: the researcher can be saved much needless frustration by the presence of a scale.

iv *Reference books*, not in themselves necessarily either rare or expensive (though frequently both) will of course be needed as support material for the rare books which form the backbone of the collection, and should be housed with it. The kind of material will naturally depend on the scope of the collection. If one assumes that for the sake of example that it is rich in incunabula, it would obviously be vital that such works as the *British Museum catalogue of fifteenth century books*, the *Gesamtkatalog der Wiegendruck*, Haebler's *Typenrepertorium*, the Hellingas' *XVth century printing types of the low countries* and so forth should be immediately to hand for the readers to use with the incunables. It would be very desirable also that the library's sets of such serials as the *Gutenberg Jahrbuch* and *The library* which are of outstanding importance for the subject should also be housed in the rare book room.

v *Other materials*: Rare book collections in the course of time tend to acquire some materials which are more museum pieces than the normal contents of the library. They may be perfectly proper as a part of its collections: one would not for a moment suggest that the Eric Gill sculptures in the Clark Library at Los Angeles are not a useful adjunct to its Gill collections, nor that Birmingham Reference Library should not have its slate-engraving by John Baskerville. The question is, how far should the library go in this museum capacity? That Loughborough Technical College has with its collection of the working papers of the Vine Press the wood-engraved blocks used to illustrate its books obviously enriches the collection from the point of view of bibliographical research. The Vine Press had no proprietary typeface, but it did have some special sorts cut for use in one of its books to replace the normal types of the commercially available typeface. The drawings for these special sorts, and the correspondence relating to them form a useful part of the collection: would the Monotype matrices, and the type themselves, also do so?(13)

It is difficult to draw up a hard and fast rule for such cases. Some museum items undoubtedly add to the research value of the collection. If one were, say, developing a collection devoted to the artist John Farleigh one would surely add to to his drawings, sketches and prints not only his wood-engraved blocks but also his engraving tools should the opportunity present itself. A certain amount of such acquisition, even when not strictly necessary for research purposes, can be extraordinarily useful for exhibition purposes; at times that will be sufficient justification. The librarian will seldom search as purposefully for such materials as he will for the more normal additions to his stock, but he will surely acquire some.

References
   1 The Library of Congress' appointment of subject consultants is

one way in which this can be done.

2 Even this is going to be more specific than will be possible for some categories of material being sought, eg fine bindings or printed ephemera, for which much more general guidelines have to suffice.

3 My pleasant personal experience has been to receive a quotation, at a very modest price, for a book I had asked Blackwells to seek, over four years after the original request.

4 In some instances it would however be reasonable to use agents in different countries at the same time, if the material is of a kind which might reasonably be found in any of them. In such cases it would be courteous and helpful to let the agents know that the others have also been asked to search.

5 A good example is the collection of materials on writing and manuscripts formed by Robert Curzon, Lord Zouche, which was deposited in the British Museum after his death in 1873, and passed into their ownership on the death of Baroness Zouche in 1917.

6 No doubt when Richard Smyth bestowed an incunable on Dr Barlow 'then cheife library keeper' at the Bodleian, as described in Chapter 1 note 19, Barlow was suitably grateful in conversation and letter, but he failed in his duty to record the gift in the donor's book. In normal cases, when the gift is useful but of no extraordinary market value a letter of thanks plus the use of a bookplate recording the source of the gift (if such accords with the library's practice) and a record of the donation in the annual report or whatever other publications are appropriate in the structure of that library, will constitute the only payment which needs to be made for what may be very valuable accessions to the stock. If the gift is of a substantial number of volumes, or of considerable monetary value, other considerations obtain, and the price may well include the production of a special catalogue, the organisation of a special exhibition, the special housing of the material and so forth.

7 *Report* 52, para 166.

8 Indeed, the sales of parts of their stock by research libraries in recent years, returning to the market place books in areas in which the libraries feel unable to concentrate, is in part inspired by the wish to avoid such unused museum pieces, and to make them available to

other libraries.

9 As an instance, a few years ago the research papers of a botanist who had spent his career in the Botanical Survey of India were offered by his executors to two institutions prominent in the field. One responded by return of post, offering to send somebody down to sort through the material in which they expressed keen interest; the other (very much nearer) replied a fortnight later asking that a list of the material be sent them so that they could select any items of interest. Needless to say, the collection went to the first institution. The second lost not only this material, but also any chance at all of being offered another collection with which one of the executors was concerned. Possibly also others, since the executor naturally told the story to others working in the field.

10 The late Sir Sydney Cockerell was pre-eminent in obtaining donations. Wilfred Blunt's *Cockerell* London, H Hamilton, 1964, is well worth studying for its account of his technique.

11 Some amusing instances of librarians' failure to take as much care as they should are given in John R Hetherington's 'Signatures and sizes' in the *Times literary supplement* 14 October 1965, p 928.

12 For the librarian who has to provide full-size print-outs for his clients, for which positive film is needed. For the reader dealing with manuscript material written in a difficult hand, negative microfilm is a nightmare.

13 Had this material formed part of the collection as purchased it would undoubtedly have been retained. As it did not do so, it was rightly felt that its purely museum value did not justify ordering it.

Chapter V
Processing, cataloguing and classification

That many of those concerned with rare material regard librarians as the natural enemies of books is due in no small part to the damage wreaked in the normal library methods of processing. It is vital to the organisation of a rare books department that the library's standard methods of acquisition and technical processing be bypassed so that the special needs of the department may be met.

So bald a statement needs justification. It is to be found on three grounds: in the first place, because of the rarity (and frequently the high market value) of accessions to a special collection there is need for greater security than with the general run of a library's purchases. Secondly, it is very important that such accessions be collated immediately upon receipt in the library, and only the staff of the special collection are likely to have the qualifications to do this. And finally, because of the library's responsibility for conservation of the material and because much of the older books acquired will be in need of attention before they can go on to the shelves, these books need to be handled more gently and examined more critically than can reasonably be expected if they are given the same treatment as the routine additions to the library's stock.

In collating the material, the librarian's basic task is to see that it corresponds with the description of the item in the auction or bookseller's catalogue from which it was ordered. A secondary, but no less important duty, is to check with bibliographies and other appropriate authorities to see that the book matches up to the descriptions there. (In the case of material received other than by purchase, this collation against the best bibliographical description available is clearly of similar importance). Dealers can make mistakes, and it is a possibility that one will obtain, say, not the first issue of a certain first edition but one in a later (but equally genuine) publishers' casing, or one lacking an errata slip called for in the bibliographies. Some of these differences will be matters which one will wish to take up with the dealer, as certainly will be such things as damage caused the book by inadequate packing—and for this purpose it is necessary that the staff of the special collection shall have seen the book in its packing at the earliest opportunity.

An area in which one may find that the bookseller's description and the actual volume differ is in condition. It is not often that one will be misled so grossly that one will wish to take the matter up with the dealer: few will describe a tired, battered copy as being very good and charge for it as though it were. But all descriptions of condition are subjective, and the terms used incapable of very precise definition. One will note, when collating new stock, that books described by a certain bookseller as very good are in no more than average second-hand condition in one's own scale of values, and be aware of this when considering books for purchase in the future.

As well as collating the new acquisitions against the standard descriptions and the bookseller's catalogue, the rare books librarian can also examine them with an eye to subsequent cataloguing purposes. To a much greater extent than is true for the library as a whole, in a special collection one is dealing with books which are in some respects unique, and this further side to collation is concerned with the unique features of the individual volumes—with the book as artifact and not just as vehicle for the text. The presence of manuscript notes, of bookplates and so forth may well be of importance to establish provenance. Since all collating takes a good deal of time, it is an economy if the examination for acquisition purposes and for cataloguing can be combined. In practice this often cannot be managed; in any case a dated and initialled record of the collation should always be marked (lightly, in pencil) in the volume to indicate that the work has been done.

Marking books
It is assumed that in common with the other additions to a library's stock, its rare books will be assigned accession numbers if such are used. In addition, they will also need marks of ownership. For the application of these ownership marks, however, a different policy is required for rare material. There is the argument, quite legitimately

advanced, that because ownership stamps and so forth detract from the appearance and the market value of the book they should be avoided. On the other hand this increases the temptation for the would-be thief, increases the difficulty of identifying the copy once it has been stolen and therefore renders restitution of a strayed copy much harder. Whatever the private collector may wish to do, the library has the duty to those who provide its funds clearly to mark all books and documents coming into its ownership. For valuable material, such marks need to be extended to those easily removed parts (such as maps and coloured plates) which are a particular temptation to the thief unless so marked. However, because of their deleterious effect such marks must be applied with discretion.

Visible marks of ownership discourage but do not prevent theft, and many of them can be removed or disguised. For this reason some libraries like also to apply secret or inconspicuous marks of ownership, a measure which can be of great value in establishing legal title to an item which has been stolen. The problems and methods of marking books were discussed very thoroughly by a Joint Working Party of the Antiquarian Booksellers Association and the Rare Books Group of the Library Association which was set up in 1972 to consider the problem of book thefts. Their report very efficiently summarises current thought on the best practice: a substantial part of this report, through the courtesy of the two bodies, is included as an appendix.

Cataloguing
It is assumed that material in a library's special collections will be catalogued in accordance with the library's routine policy for its stock, at any rate in all those instances in which the material is amenable to such cataloguing. Though separately housed and administered, it is entirely appropriate that all users of the library should be assisted in access to its rare books through the normal guides which the library provides to its stock.

With such normal library cataloguing we are not here concerned, but rather with the special cataloguing and description which will be required by the nature of the special collection and the purposes of those who use it.

As has been indicated, not all materials in special collections are amenable to 'normal' cataloguing at all. Writing to his friend Strickland Gibson about his collection of printed ephemera now in the Bodleian Library, John Johnson wrote '. . . There were many dangers to be overcome not so much in the preoccupations of collecting as in the technique of mounting, of housing, cataloguing and much else.'

There is a not uninteresting proof of this. Some years ago a director of the Huntington Museum of California came to Europe to see what Europe was doing on this side of things. He went to Germany and drew blank. He went to London and drew blank, but in London somebody happened to mention Oxford and my name and he came here and settled down to study what we were trying to do. At the end he gave it as his opinion that the principal reason why we appeared to have some prospect of success was that we had broken clean away from all library technique which could not be adapted to such a purpose as this. In his opinion only those standing outside library technique and viewing the problem from a detached and experimental point of view had a chance of success. For instance, a library's card index of such a collection would be as big as the collection itself.'

Though the John Johnson collection of printed ephemera at Bodley is scarcely typical, many special collections contain materials which equally demand a different treatment. Because it forms such a commonplace part of collections, one tends to forget that manuscript material—collections of letters, for instance—is just such a category in which standard library technique is inadequate. For archival material, where the fundamental principle is *respect des fonds*, the sanctity of the archive group, the ordinary methods of librarianship are quite unsuitable. In the inventorising, calendaring and indexing of such material the normal practice to be followed is that of the archivist. (1)

For other kinds of material forming part of a rare book collection special cataloguing will normally take its form from the purposes of those who use the collection—although this is a circular affair, the use made of the collection inevitably being affected by the extent to which methods of access to it are supplied.

In general the librarian charged with the responsibility of developing catalogues of a special collection needs to approach his material more in the manner of a bibliographer than of the librarian applying the standard techniques and codes of his profession. There are conventions of description and arrangement which one will normally follow, naturally, but these should not have the binding force that will prevail in other branches of library work. One must adopt a more empirical approach: if some conventions are ill-suited to the particular case of the collection and its users they may be modified or disregarded.

'How is the material going to be used?' is the question the rare books librarian must ask. It should be emphasised that this question is not limited in scope to those consulting the catalogues within the institution. It must also consider the wider aspects of publicity for the collection and of its use by those outside the institution. Although the publication of the catalogue is of very limited use until the collection has grown to respectable size in its given field of interest, the publication of catalogues (whether of the whole or of parts of the collection) is an important part of the function of the rare books librarian, and provides a way in which the needs of distant scholars can be served very usefully. In deciding how the collection is likely to be used the librarian naturally consider such long-distance use as well as internal requirements; the answer will indicate the arrangement and contents of the catalogues.

In fact many rare book collections consist of several distinct parts. The William Andrews Clark Library at UCLA, for instance, has special collections in 17th and 18th century English cultural life, in Oscar Wilde and the 90s, in Montana history and in modern fine printing. Such an array of subjects is by no means unusual, and should sufficiently show that a catalogue of the 'rare book collection' as such cannot be of much more use than as a shelf-location aid, and for such a purpose 'normal' library cataloguing will often be adequate. What is needed is a series of catalogues for each of the special parts of the collection, in each instance being compiled according to the needs inherent in those particular books and the research patterns of those who use them.

Cataloguing the contents of a special collection, then, is of three kinds: first the routine cataloguing as a part of the whole library;

secondly the production of special catalogues of parts of the collection, designed for internal use by the staff and readers in the rare book library; and finally the production of catalogues for publication. Although the arrangement and content of entries in these published catalogues (as also, of course, in exhibition catalogues) may well differ in some respects from those in the second category, it is desirable that they should in most cases be edited from the entries in the unpublished catalogues, the distinction being in the provision of introductory explanatory matter, arrangement and annotation rather than in the bulk of information contained.

In some instances, very full cataloguing is desirable, in which full-dress bibliographical descriptions will be needed according to the precepts of Greg, Bowers, Stevenson, Tanselle and Gaskell.(2) The rigour of descriptive bibliography will naturally be the exception and employed normally only in those libraries pre-eminent in a particular field and in which the catalogue descriptions serve as a substitute for a formal bibliography.

The *British Museum catalogue of fifteenth century books* and the *Catalogue of the Hunt Botanical Library* (figures 1 and 2) will serve as examples of such formal catalogues of rare book collections. Having been conceived more than three-quarters of a century ago, *BMC*'s bibliographical style does not altogether accord with formulae later developed for the description of early printed books, but is a model of scholarly cataloguing at its best. The Hunt Catalogue is much more recent, and in its cataloguing extends the Greg Bowers method of bibliographical description (which had been devised with English literary texts in mind) to take account of some of the special problems inherent in botanical books with coloured plates which are often the most important part of the book. A particularly valuable feature of this catalogue, in fact, is in Allan Stevenson's 'A bibliographical method for the description of botanical books' printed on pages cxli–ccxxxi of volume 2 part 1 of the catalogue. Undeservedly neglected, this section explains the function and importance of the various elements in a way which can be appreciated by the botanical reader as well as by the bibliographer. (3)

Both these catalogues, it should be noted, are arranged in a 'natural

MIGUEL ALBERT

DATES. The text type of the Repertorium de prauitate haereticorum, 16 September, 1494 (IB. 52018), attributable on documentary evidence to the press of Miguel Albert, who also edited the text, is used also in an unsigned edition of Juan Roig, De patre non incarnato, Valencia, 1494 (Haebler 582; Vindel, vol. 3, p. 111, no. 49). These seem to be the only works to be assigned to Albert as printer, though he is known from documentary evidence to have commissioned work from other printers at Valencia at the same period (cf. Introduction, p. xlix above).

TYPES (see Plate VII[S]):
104 G. [P., Palmart 3*], text type previously used by Palmart [P. 3], but here distinguishable by certain capitals different from those used in Pérez de Valentia, Expositio in Cantica Canticorum, Palmart, 19 May, 1486 (IB. 52014), namely C and E large, with stem sloping; N with straight shanks, Q small, empty; S large, plain, with medial hook. Though not observed in the above-mentioned Pérez, Expositio, D small, double-shouldered, and V with inner hook, used in the Repertorium, are shown in the facsimile of Pomponius Mela, Palmart, 1482, in Vindel, vol. 3, p. 30. Majuscule N of Palmart's type is used for H in the Repertorium. The shoulder of minuscule h is lower than in Palmart 104 G.

150 G. [P., Palmart 4], heading type in the Lyonnese style, resembling Petrus Ungarus (Lyons) 155 G. [P. 2]. Many of the capitals double-shanked and/or double-crossed. I scrolled. The upper and lower curves of diamonded S are detached from the central curve. Haebler's M[96], in two parts, the left double-shanked and double-crossed. Indistinguishable from Hagenbach and Hutz 150 G. [P. 2; Haebler 4], De la Roca 150 G. [Haebler 3, Typographie ibérique, no.s 67, 68], and Rosenbach (Barcelona) 150 G. [Haebler 9, Gesellschaft für Typenkunde 663].

*** Haebler's type 3 (Bibliografía ibérica, pt. 2, p. 247) is not represented in the Museum collection. The unsigned edition of Juan Boix, Tractatus conceptuum, 8 February, 1493, in which it occurs (Haebler 61; Vindel, vol. 8, pp. 385–6), was apparently commissioned but not printed by Albert (cf. Introduction, p. xlix, n. 4, above).

REPERTORIUM. Repertorium perutile de prauitate haereticorum. [Edited by Miguel Albert.] 16 September, 1494.

2[a]. (headline) Prologus. ||| In noïe dñi nostri iesu || xp̄i oē qǒcūq3 facim̄[9] v́bo aut ope .ī || noïe dñi iesu xp̄i facere debem̄[9] ... 2[b], col. 1, l. 10: a Biuratio Primo || sciendum est ꝗ heretici||... 301[b], col. 2, l. 8, COLOPHON: Explicit reportorium perutile de || prauitate hereticorum et apostata⸗|| rum summa cura ac diligētia exami||natum emendatumq3 per prestātis||simum virum ingenij clarissimū iu⸗||ris vtriusq3 interpretem ac doctorē || famosum Michaelem albert valen||tinum: in nobili ciuitate Valentina. || Impressum Anno a natiuitate dñi || M. cccc. lxxxxiiij. die v́o decimase⸗||xta mensis septembris.

Folio. a[8] b–e[8] f[4] g[8] h–z[8] z[10] A–M[8] N O[10]. 302 leaves, the first and last blank. 2 columns. 2[a]: 38 lines and headline, 198 (212)× 138 mm. Types: 150 G., headlines, headings; 104 G. Capital spaces, some with guide-letters. Haebler 573. Vindel, vol. 3, p. 108, no. 48. Hain 13875.

An agreement for the printing of 1,000 copies of this book was entered into on 12 September, 1493, between Dr. Miguel Albert and Juan Gómez de Çarrión, 'Receptor de las penas del Santo Oficio', the paper to be provided by Gómez, and the cost of printing by Albert. Type and matrices were purchased by Albert from Lambert Palmart on 21 November of the same year (Serrano y Morales, pp. 3, 4).

In this as in other copies, leaf D 3 has been cut away, while a slip of paper (later removed) has been pasted over the first 9 lines of text on the following page. The passage, omitted in the edition of 1575 ('apud D. Zenarum', Venice), was no doubt suppressed by the Censor.

280×200 mm. Imperfect, wanting sheet G 4, in place of which is bound a duplicate of sheet G 3. Without the blanks. Bound after IB. 52862 (Gundisaluus de Villadiego, Tractatus contra haereticam prauitatem, Hutz and Sanz, Salamanca, 1496) q.v.

Bought in June, 1896.   IB. 52018.

Plate 1:   Part of a page from the *British Museum catalogue of 15th century books* showing a typical entry.

1766

592 LOCKE, John (1632–1704), English philosopher.

Observations upon the Growth and Culture of Vines and Olives. London 1766. Foolscap 8°.

OBSERVATIONS UPON | THE GROWTH AND CULTURE | OF VINES AND OLIVES: | THE PRODUCTION OF SILK: | THE PRESERVATION OF FRUITS. | WRITTEN AT THE REQUEST OF | THE EARL OF SHAFTESBURY: | TO WHOM IT IS INSCRIBED. | BY Mʳ. JOHN LOCKE. | NOW FIRST PRINTED FROM THE | ORIGINAL MANUSCRIPT IN | THE POSSESSION OF THE | PRESENT EARL OF | SHAFTESBURY. | LONDON: | PRINTED FOR W. SANDBY, IN FLEET STREET. | M DCC LXVI.

COLLATION: 8°: Aˣ(–A₁) B:Eˣ Fˣ(–F6): iii:xv [i] 1–73 [1]. A1ᵛ⎕, missing, A2: title, vⒹ. A3: 'THE EDITOR | TO THE READER', signed at Temple, March 1766, 'G. S'. A7: dedication to Anthony [Ashley Cooper, first] Earl of Shaftesbury, signed at Christ Church, Feb. 1675, 'JOHN LOCKE'. A8ᵛ⎕. B1: text, headed below two double rules 'WINE'. C4ᵛⒹ. C5: 'OIL'. E2ᵛⒹ. E3: 'FRUIT'. E8: 'SILK'. F5ᵛ (colophon between rules): 'PRINTED BY RICHARDSON AND CLARK, | IN FLEET STREET, LONDON.' F6ᵛ⎕, missing. No RTs.

PAPER: Pro Patria, Dutch, fine, marked Maid of Holland | G [bell] R = I V and wreath within circle. Leaf 6.15 x 3.8″ = sheet [13 x 17'].

TYPE: Small pica roman much leaded 58: B2 = 20 lines. Preface: english roman much leaded 66+: A5 = 17 lines. Dedication: great primer roman much leaded 99: A7ᵛ = 11 lines.

BINDING: Old polished calf with narrow floral blind-stamped borders. Heraldic bookplate of William Gilstrap.

REFERENCES: Lowndes; BM, DA, MH-A, MBHₒ, Lind, Rath.

NOTES: This small work was a fruit of Locke's sojourn in France in 1675–79. Many of the philosopher's writings were collected for the edition of 1714, but the publication of this piece was delayed for a half century more. The capitals in the main title are slightly spread.

The editor, 'G. S.', remembering Locke's association with the government of Carolina, sees in Locke's *Observations* a number applicable to horticulture in America, and imagines that the consequent commerce in silk, wines, and olives will induce the 'most perfect harmony ... between Great Britain and her colonies'.

Though Lowndes correctly lists the little book as 'small 8vo.', such recent lists as MH-A, MBHₒ, and Lindley call it 16°. The volume has vertical chains and is the natural result of folding Pro Patria (foolscap) sheets in 8°.

The printers named in the colophon were William Richardson, nephew of Samuel Richardson, and his partner Samuel Clarke, the Quaker printer.

1766–68

593 LINNAEUS, Carl (1707–1778), Swedish naturalist.

Systema naturæ per regna tria naturæ. 12th ed. Stockholm 1766–68. 3 vols. in 4. *Medium* 8°.

CAROLI A LINNÉ, [II:III: LINNÉ] | *Equitis Aur. de Stella Polari,* [II:III: EQUIT. AURAT. DE STELLA POLARI,] | ARCHIATRI REGII, MED. & BOTAN. PROFESS. UPSAL., [II:III *omit line*] | ACAD. PARIS. UPSAL. HOLMENS. PETROPOL. [II:III: ACAD. PARIS. MONSP. &c.] | BEROL. IMPER. LOND. ANGL. MONSPEL. [II:III *omit*] | TOLOS. FLORENT. EDINB. BERN. SOC. [II:III *omit*] | S Y S T E M A | N A T U R Æ | PER | REGNA TRIA NATURÆ, | SECUNDUM | CLASSES, ORDINES, | GENERA, SPECIES, | CUM [II: CUM] | CHARACTERIBUS, DIFFERENTIIS, | [II:III: CHARACTERIBUS & DIFFERENTIIS,] | SYNONYMIS, LOCIS. [II:III *omit*] | TOMUS I. [II.] [III.] | ——— [III *omit*] | EDITIO DUODECIMA, REFORMATA. [III *omit*] | ——— | *Cum Privilegio Sᵃ:æ Rᵉ:æ Mᵗᵗⁱ Sueciæ* [II:III: ...] & *Electoris Saxon.* | [III *only:* ~~~~~] | ⊂⊃⊂⊃⊂⊃ | H O L M I Æ, [II: HOLMIÆ,] | IMPENSIS DIRECT. LAURENTII SALVII, | 1766. [1767: 1768.]

[Vol. I, Pt. 2] CAROLI A LINNÉ | *S Y S T E M A* | *N A T U R Æ.* | TOM. I. PARS II. | ——— | EDITIO DUODECIMA REFORMATA. | [row of small fleurons] | *H O L M I Æ,* | IMPENSIS DIRECT. LAUR. SALVII, 1767.

COLLATION: 8°: Vol. I (Pt. 1): Aˣ(±A1) B–Kˣ 2Lˣ (A2 unsigned); [iv] 5:10 11–532 (37+75 as '274':'275'). A1: title. A1ᵛ: quotation, *Psalms,* CIII: 24. A2: dedication to Count Carl G. Tessin, dated 'Upsaliæ 1766,' d. 24 Maji, signed 'C. a Linné.' A3: 'RATIO EDITIONIS,' dated 'Upsaliæ 1766.' A4ᵛ: 'INTROITUS.'

Plate 2:   Two pages from the *Hunt botanical catalogue* showing a full entry.

history' order designed to illustrate the growth of the literature, and not in author or subject sequences: *BMC* in 'Proctor order' and the Hunt Catalogue in a straight chronological sequence. Such a primary arrangement of the catalogue may not be found best on many occasions, perhaps, but it has many virtues in subjects which attract historical research, and the need for a chronological index to catalogues arranged in another way should not be overlooked. The present writer would have been spared the drudgery of constructing his own chronological arrangements on more than a few occasions had more libraries provided such an index!

The distinction between catalogues of the *BMC*/Hunt kind and the full-dress bibliography is relatively slight. As they describe the copies of books in their respective collections rather than the 'ideal copy' of the bibliography, the entries are sometimes slightly shorter. But, as the examples show very clearly, they are anything but instances of compact, economical cataloguing. The Hunt catalogue, it will be noted, includes details on paper, plates, type and binding as well as the quasifacsimile transcription, collation, references and notes—in such detail that entries for the more important and copiously illustrated books will extend over several pages. The costs of such cataloguing are enormous; the costs of printing equally so. Few libraries will be able to undertake such elaborate work save for very restricted sections of their collections. Even in the Hunt catalogue, in the production of which economics loomed less largely than usual, works regarded as of minor importance were perfectly reasonably described in briefer form.

The shorter form that this will take naturally depends also on the nature of the collection. In the Manchester Reference Library's *Subject catalogue, Section 094: Private press books* 2 vols, Manchester 1959–60 dealing as it does with a category of library material in which interest is usually in the presses rather more than in the authors or subjects of the books printed, it was useful to arrange the catalogue alphabetically under the names of the presses, with a chronological sequence under each for the books it had printed. No attempt was made at a bibliographer's description of the books listed(4) but close attention to their physical production was a useful feature of the catalogue.

This physical description was much briefer than has since become the pattern with, for instance, the Private Libraries Association's annual checklists *Private press books*, but is by no means without value, particularly since the catalogue refers by convenient symbols to the fuller descriptions given in various bibliographies which had previously been published, both collective and of individual presses. The indexes given (of authors, illustrators and of binders) are adequate for most of the purposes required of a catalogue, though falling short of the requirements which might be specified today.(5)

As a second example of the catalogue of intermediate size it is useful to consider Robert H MacDonald's *The library of Drummond of Hawthornden* Edinburgh, 1971. This is, admittedly, to stretch the point, since Dr MacDonald's work is not properly to be regarded as the catalogue of a rare book collection. However, it provides an excellent instance of the research built around an individual's library, and forms a union catalogue of books which formerly belonged to Drummond. As such, it illustrates many of the points and problems which relate to libraries which contain distinct or distinguishable collections for which old catalogues exist.

A feature of the more extensive catalogues of rare book collections is the wealth of information they provide as a service to scholarship, not only in the body of the catalogue entries but also in the prefatory matter. The value of the introductory essays at the beginning of each volume of *BMC* should need no stressing; similarly in the Hunt Catalogue the addition of various long studies (like John S Fulton on medical aspects of early botanical books in volume 1, or that by Allan Stevenson already referred to) contributes powerfully to the value of the catalogues as reference works of far more importance than the straight unadorned catalogue could have been.

In the case of *The library of Drummond of Hawthornden* to write of 'prefatory matter' is a distinctly inadequate way to treat of the one hundred and forty pages of study of the growth of Drummond's collection and the surveys of the various subject fields contained in it. Dr MacDonald in his introduction described Drummond's catalogue as 'a slice of intellectual history' and his examination of (for example) the theological books it contained provides one of the best succinct studies available of the growth of ideas and the kinds of books available in the period.

Rare book librarians will seldom have the opportunity to spread themselves in this way in their more general catalogues (though it is to be hoped that in more limited areas, for exhibition catalogues and the like, they will provide such evaluative guides) but it is an approach which should not be ignored since it is by such methods that much of the information known to the specialist and which is otherwise 'locked up' in the catalogue entries, can be made available to the less advanced student.

In an article in *The library* at the beginning of this century James Duff Brown attacked the work of his bibliographer contemporaries in no uncertain terms, proclaiming their work 'to be little better than a hollow sham.' Though rightly trounced by A W Pollard's reply in the same issue, Brown had a valid point when he asked 'Can any one of the learned bibliographers who have wasted years collecting title-pages and collations, and even specimens, just give us a glimmer of light on the contents of the books which interested people of the fifteenth century? What were their popular poetry, fiction, philosophy, art, and other studies?' The bibliography (or catalogue) which is simply a bibliography is to some extent a wasted opportunity; certainly the value of published catalogues is considerably enhanced when the users are given 'a glimmer of light' in this way.

In compiling the catalogue of Drummond's library, Dr MacDonald followed (with modifications) Drummond's own practice of arranging the books by language and subject: a departure from the systems of arrangement which will normally be adopted, but in this instance appropriate. Thus the arrangement is of Latin books on theology, on philosophy, on law and so on, followed by Greek books, Hebrew books and other language divisions. In each group for convenience the compiler has adopted an alphabetical author arrangement, following British Museum practice on names, except that when seventeenth century common usage demanded another form he followed that usage. 'It seemed sensible' he wrote 'to call Ramus "Ramus" rather than conceal him under the name of "La Ramée" . . .' Those who have laboured under the difficulties imposed on users of catalogues of

early printed books by the cataloguing codes will applaud this victory for common sense.

And it is a common sense catalogue, as well as a scholarly one. 'I have quoted titles at some length' wrote Dr MacDonald, 'because this is one way of keeping the "flavour" of the books—besides, much useful information is given in these long-winded titles; the bias or religion of the author, the name of the pamphlet he is replying to, the audience he is hoping to reach. Even the purely honorific salutations tell us something about the age . . . I have not meddled with spelling or punctuation, but reproduced titles with as little modification as possible, short of breaking into bibliographers' quasi-facsimile . . . With imprints, I have taken some bibliographical liberties. I have translated printers' names as much as possible into the vernacular, and I have done the same with place names. Only bibliographers will know that Rothomagnum is Rouen . . .'.

A typical entry from the catalogue, taken from the section on English Books, reads

> Mentries Tragedies   [Eng. 6]
> 698   Alexander William, Earl of Stirling
> The monarchicke tragedies. Croesus,
> Darius, The Alexandraean, Iulius Caesar.
> Newly enlarged. 4° London, V. Simmes
> for E.Blount, 1607.
> STC 344. Greg 209, 196, 260, 261   NLS
> Heavily annotated by Drummond

It is virtually a short-title catalogue entry, with an appropriate identification number in the catalogue, reference to the location of the entry in Drummond's manuscript catalogue, reference to the entries in standard bibliographies, and to the present location of the copy. For the aims of the catalogue, no more is needed other than the indexing provided in the alphabetical author index.

Very much briefer, in one sense, is H M Adams's *Catalogue of books printed on the continent of Europe 1501–1600, in Cambridge libraries* (Cambridge, 1967). It is unlike the examples already cited, in being a union catalogue of material in more than thirty Cambridge libraries, in being almost completely the work of one man, and in its thirty thousand titles covering a much wider range of material.

As it is a union catalogue, short-title entries were obviously appropriate, as was the adoption of an alphabetical author arrangement. Typical entries are

291 **Heraldus, Desiderius.** Aduersariorum libri
duo. pp.183. à^8 A–M^8. 8°. Parisiis, apud
Ieremiam Perier, 1599. C. (2) Tr. Cla. Pet.

59 **Ramus, Johannes.** Ad Iustianum de tutelis
libri duo. pp.85. a–f^8. 8°. Louanii, excud.
(ex off.) Bartholomaeus Grauius. 1557. TH.

These entries, it will be noted, include the union catalogue's own reference numbers.(7) The headings usefully follow the same practice as in the Drummond catalogue of using the older style of name; although being very sensibly modelled upon Cambridge University Library practice there are also form entries under such headings as Liturgies, and quite a number of vernacular names (Geoffrey of Monmouth, for instance, appears as Geoffrey and not as Galfridus *Monumetensis*). The catalogue entries differ from many short-title catalogues in giving a rather full statement of imprint, and also by collating the signatures. Both additions will have added very considerably to the compiler's work, but also very much to the value of the catalogue. By examining personally every copy of every book recorded, Dr Adams avoided some of the serious errors into which reliance on existing catalogues would have led him: ' . . . One library catalogue said it had three copies of a particular book. These I found were all printed in the same place at the same date. But in the imprint were three different names. As the catalogue in question, in common with almost all the Cambridge catalogues, never mentions a printer or publisher, the three volumes were indistinguishable in it, though in fact all different.'

Adam's catalogue includes two other features which make it a particularly useful reference book, in common with the British Museum's short-title catalogues of Italian and German books, whose example he followed by the inclusion of two indexes of printers. The first is arranged alphabetically under their names, and (after noting their place of work) lists the books they printed in chronological order. The second is an alphabetical arrangement of place names (with, of course, references from different forms eg from 'Alcalá' to 'Compluti') and under each a simple chronological listing of those who printed or published there. The importance of lists of this kind is well recognised by bibliographers, but they are still regrettably often lacking in the cataloguing of rare book collections.

These examples sufficiently show the variety of approach needed in the cataloguing of rare material. It is cataloguing for *use*; cataloguing dictated by the form and content of the collection and by the ways in which the researcher will use it. It may be argued(8) that the physical arrangement of the material on the shelves makes some of these special catalogues or indexes superfluous: that if the books are arranged chronologically, a chronological index implies duplication of effort to no good purpose, for example. This, and the other criticisms which may be voiced about the heavy cost of such specialised cataloguing, appears to me first to overlook the fact that the books will be in stock a very long time, and one surely ought to reckon the costs against the period of time for which one is cataloguing an item for use. Secondly they apparently ignore one of the principal objectives of the rare book collection: the preservation of materials which are not expendable. Any device of cataloguing which reduces needless handling of the collection contributes to its preservation. If additionally it can provide a particular tool of research for the distant scholar that is an added benefit.

This, of course, is to recommend the ideal, and we do not live in an ideal world in which unpleasant questions of economics and cost-effectiveness play no part. One has to compromise, and in many cases can do so by adopting an abbreviated form when a satisfactory full-dress form is already available in one of the standard bibliographies or catalogues (to which, of course, one's own short entry would make reference). In those instances when one's own copy is a variant of that described in a bibliography it is still often practicable to utilise a brief entry, indicating the ways in which the copy differs from that in the printed description.

Subject cataloguing and classification

I have suggested above that material in the rare book collection will be catalogued and classified in accordance with the library's normal policies, and that the special cataloguing will be undertaken as an additional function. However, it is worth considering the extent to which routine subject cataloguing and/or classification is really justified for

There is, to be sure, considerable advantage in theory if all the library's resources are made available for recall through the use of these routine methods. The advantage will often be a very real one, but this will depend very much on the period, scope and content of the special collection and upon the kind of subject cataloguing and classification used in the library. Even if one ignores such special cases as the John Johnson collection at Bodley, one can without difficulty think of many special collections for which the application of such routine processing will be extraordinarily difficult, and of little practical value. The crux of the matter, of course, is in the changes in the way in which men have thought, and organised their knowledge in written and printed form.(9) To attempt, for example, the close organisation of a collection of early 17th century theology according to 19th or 20th century ideas of classification will be a frustrating and largely useless exercise. It is of course excellent if it is found helpful to arrange the special collection according to the general classification scheme used, and to have subject entries for its materials in the main catalogues. But often other arrangements either of books or of catalogue entries will be found superior.

References

1 As described in such standard books as T R Schellenberg, *The management of archives* New York, 1965, or Sir Hilary Jenkinson's *A manual of archive administration* 2nd rev ed London, 1937, offset litho reprint 1965.

2 Given in Fredson Bowers *Principles of bibliographical description* Princeton 1949; Philip Gaskell *A new introduction to bibliography* Oxford, 1972; Allan Stevenson 'A bibliographical method for the description of botanical books' in *Catalogue of botanical books in the collection of Rachel*

McMasters Hunt Pittsburgh 1961, vol 2 part 1 pp cxli–ccxxxi. Tanselle's extensions of Bowers's methods have been published in a series of papers in *The library* and elsewhere; they are conveniently listed in Gaskell pp 412–3. As a corrective, David Foxon's *Thoughts on the history and future of bibliographical description* Los Angeles, 1970, is particularly useful. R B McKerrow's *An introduction to bibliography for literary students* Oxford 1927, and Sir Walter Greg's 'A formulary of collation' reprinted in his *Collected papers* Oxford 1966 pp 298–313, still remain classics in the field.

3 By no means all users of catalogues will be bibliographers, and the inclusion of such an explanation will frequently be a valuable adjunct.

4 With the exception of Alan Hazen's classic study of the Strawberry Hill Press, no real bibliographical account of private press work has in fact been attempted.

5 Recent issues of *Private press books*, for instance, have specified press used, whether the paper was damped before printing, and so forth. This tendency towards elaboration of descriptions is very common; whether it can really be justified is questionable.

6 *The library* new series, vol 4 (1903) pp 144–62.

7 These are complete only with the initial prefixed (H291, R59): a point which librarians have not always noted with Wing, who used the same system.

8 As John E Alden seems to argue on p 72 of his excellent survey of 'Cataloguing and classification' in *Rare book collections* ed by H Richard Archer, Chicago, 1965. (ACRL Monograph 27).

9 A good account of some of the problems—from the viewpoint of consulting old catalogues—is given on pp 154–5 of Archer Taylor's *Book catalogues: their varieties and uses*, Chicago, 1957.

Chapter VI
The care and restoration of rare books

Readers of Victorian novels have a clear idea of the problems presented by the entailed estate. The inheritor of such, it was very well recognised a century ago, was in morality as in law no more than a life tenant, charged with the responsibility for maintaining the fabric, replanting the timber trees and so forth, so that when the property passed to his heirs it was in at least as good state as when it came into his possession. Our grandfathers understood all about it, in a way which is becoming increasingly difficult in an age of built-in obsolescence.

The librarian who takes charge of a special collection is in very much the position of the Victorian heir. The collections under his charge are for the use of himself and his readers, but if he neglects to see that the materials are preserved for future readers' benefit, he is putting himself in the position of the wastrel who felled the timber without replanting, and posterity will judge him no more kindly than the Victorians did such reckless behaviour.

Satisfactory conservation of the stock will demand close attention to the books when they come into the special collection, not only to ensure that the book itself is sound, but also to eliminate the risk that it will be the agent of damage to other books. The care of the books, once within the collection, and the careful supervision of their use, is no less a part of conservation: the sections of the succeeding chapters which discuss this are also relevant here.

The rare books librarian himself need not, of course, be an expert in the conservation of library materials, at any rate in the sense of knowing the *precise* cause of the decay of the paper in this book, or of the deterioration of the binding on that.(1) Still less is he to be expected to remedy these defects himself; that is a matter for the skilled conservationist. The librarian with experience will be rather like a general practitioner: well able to diagnose many of the causes of a book's decay, and able to prescribe measures which will prevent or arrest some types of deterioration. But equally he will refer serious cases to a specialist, and leave the subsequent operation to that specialist.

The importance of collation of new stock added to the collection, as a routine task of the keeper of a special collection, is not limited to the purposes described in Chapter V. The librarian collates the book for conservation purposes as well as those of acquisitions and cataloguing. He must have a routine for the physical examination of the book from this point of view.

Binding

The first thing that will be examined is the binding. If it is an original binding or casing, or one contemporary with the publication, its preservation is of more importance than for, say, a nineteenth century binding on a seventeenth century book. But in any case the librarian will inspect it for the condition of the covering material, for wear in the corners, at the head and foot of the spine, along the hinges. The volume will be inspected for the state of the sewing and its tightness in the covers. The extent of damage or decay is assessed and noted, so that the measures necessary to arrest and repair it can be taken.

What action is to be taken is not simply a matter of deciding, on the condition of the binding alone, that this volume requires only cleaning, that one to have its binding restored, a third to be completely rebound and so forth. The principles that the librarian must observe are fortunately less rigorous than those which should prevail in archive work, but it is worth recalling what those are: '. . . No process of repair may be allowed to remove, diminish, falsify or obscure in any way, the document's value as evidence; and this must apply not only to the evidence obviously conveyed by the writing upon the document, but also to those overtones of evidence conveyed by it through other means . . . No process of repair may be used which could in any way damage or weaken the material of which the document is made . . . An ill-conceived method of repair, or one insufficiently tried, may prove to be a cure worse than the disease . . . Reducing all this to simple practical rules, the repairer must endeavour to put nothing into his document which was not there when he received it, and to take from it nothing which was. And before starting on a repair, he may well ask himself 'How *little* need I do to this document to make it fit for use again?' . . .(2)

This last is a question which the rare books librarian will bear constantly in mind, for excellent practical reasons. Skilled conservationists and restorers of bindings are few, and their work cannot be done cheaply. In many instances—as when a parish library of some hundreds of neglected volumes comes into one's care—the cost of refurbishing the whole collection to ideal standards will be impossibly high. To clean the bindings, to treat them with a suitable preservative dressing, and to secure to the books boards which have become detached, by tying the volumes with tape, will satisfactorily prevent further deterioration of a substantial proportion of the collection. Only a relatively small number will, in normal circumstances (that is, assuming that the books have not been exposed to damp) demand more than this first-aid.

The results will not be as pretty as if all the volumes were to be passed to a restorer for rebacking, new lettering pieces to be prepared and so forth, but they will be more truthful, and less of the 'overtones of evidence' will be concealed or destroyed. The alternative which can come to the minds of librarians unfamiliar with the idea of conservation—to send the lot to a library binder's to be reclothed in tidy modern library bindings—is too horribly inept for words.

The methods of cleaning bindings, and of treating them with suitable dressings, are described well in such guides as Carolyn Horton's *Cleaning and preserving bindings and related materials* Chicago, ALA, 1967. The rare book librarian will as a part of his training have gone beyond this, with such books as Bernard Middleton's *History of English craft bookbinding technique* London, Hafner, 1963 or his *Restoration of leather bindings* Chicago, ALA, 1972. He may well have taken elementary courses in binding himself(3) and at the very least will certainly have observed such work being done by a skilled restorer—not with the intention of undertaking repair work himself, save of the simplest kinds, but so that he is sufficiently conversant with problems and methods intelligently to request help from the specialist.

In those cases where the binding is in such a state of collapse that the volume must go for restoration, there is professional disagreement about the precise form such restoration should take. On the one hand is the archivist's viewpoint that there should be no attempt whatsoever to disguise restoration: that newly added leather should not be tooled, nor new end-leaves toned-in to match the originals. Another school of thought holds that such naked restoration is aesthetically undesirable, and that repairs should be blended in by antiquing and whatever other artifices seem suitable. Common sense and discretion on the part of the librarian and the specialist restorer will probably seek for a middle way between the two extremes: provided that the restorer includes in the volume a note of the work done, which is attached as a permanent record, there is seldom harm in attempting to retain the aesthetic integrity of the volume. But of course at times there will be conflicting factors, such as the choice between period fidelity and maximum strength, which will demand difficult decisions.

Paper

Having completed his assessment of a book's binding, the librarian will turn to a consideration of its internal condition, observing the state of the paper. In this he will be looking for both extrinsic and intrinsic causes of deterioration. The extrinsic will include wear through use (dog-eared, frayed, stained leaves), through attack by macrobiological pests (eg roaches, silverfish) or microbiological (moulds), and environmental factors (heat, light, damp, dust). If the librarian is fortunate enough to be dealing with eighteenth century or earlier books, the intrinsic causes of decay (the result of papermaking materials and methods which create a highly acid paper) will not be such an affliction as will face the curator charged with the care of cheap nineteenth or twentieth century materials.

The librarian soon learns the difference between good-quality and bad-quality papers, as he does between the different kinds of damage caused by the different macrobiological agents. Dealing with good-quality papers which have been the subject of insect attack is a straightforward problem of elimination and restoration. The librarian will be assisted in establishing the cause of such damage, whether

86

it is still active, and what he can do to control it, by such books as George Cunha's *Conservation of library materials* 2nd ed Metuchen, Scarecrow Press, 1971 or W J Plumbe's *The preservation of books in tropical and subtropical countries* Kuala Lumpur, OUP, 1964. In case of doubt, the assistance of archivists or conservationists should be sought at once.

When the paper is not in good condition but is badly decayed or brittle, either for intrinsic causes or through contamination through exposure to damp and/or microbiological attack, much more radical methods of treatment are needed, and needed urgently, since the deterioration is probably continuing. These methods may involve deacidifying, resizing, silking or laminating: all of them techniques calling for the hands of the specialist.

There are some simple methods which the librarian may himself use to test the acidity of papers which the librarian suspects are deteriorating. For laboratory work paper samples will be shredded, treated with hydroxides, and the acidity of the extract will be measured. Such a method will give very accurate results; far more accurate than is really needed by the librarian whose interest is only in the general condition of the paper—whether very acid, slightly acid, neutral or alkaline. For his purposes a wide range neutral indicator, a pH testing solution available form chemical suppliers will be perfectly adequate: a drop applied to a piece of paper will, by the colour it assumes, indicate the acidity of the fibres. Similarly, as it is often useful when considering restoration work to know whether a particular book's paper is wholly or in part made from mechanical wood, the application of a drop of Herzberg's stain will often give a crude identification of its fibre content. Linen or cotton fibres will turn the spot red, chemical wood blue and mechanical wood yellow. But the librarian may well decide to leave this testing to the experts who will have to restore the books.

A factor in the preservation of books that is of great importance, and which is too easily forgotten, is that acidity of paper is a contagious disease. The acidity introduced into a manuscript written on all-rag paper with iron-gall inks will spread from the written sheets to unwritten sheets adjacent to them; the cause of the brown mirror-

image often to be seen on seventeenth and eighteenth century manuscripts. Similarly a book which is itself printed on good paper which
has tipped into it a review printed on newsprint, or a slim pamphlet
which has been bound up into a volume with blank leaves of poor
quality to bulk it out to bindable proportions—both these are items
which have been placed at risk.

This migration of acidity is important not only for accessions to the
library, but also for the means used to store them. It is futile to worry
about the acid content of the paper in letters, maps, prints and the like
if the librarian then stores them in envelopes, folders or pamphlet
boxes made of standard modern materials which will almost certainly
have a high acid content. The librarian must take care to see that all
the materials used in the rare book collection are satisfactory from this
point of view. He can scarcely refuse to accept a new accession to the
collection on the grounds that it is made of non-lasting materials, but
he can certainly do so for the folders and boxes in which he will store
his accessions.

In considering the paper of his new stock, then, the librarian will
take all steps necessary to eliminate macrobiological or fungal attack,
whenever he finds evidence of it. In some instances, of course, reme-
dial action will already have been taken when the accession comes
from reputable booktrade sources. Their treatment will probably be
satisfactory but the methods adopted by less reputable trade sources
cannot be relied upon, and may be positively harmful. (4) To be on the
safe side, to fumigate all suspect acquisitions with thymol or formalin
vapour is wise for microbiological attack. For insect pests the use of a
fumigation chamber is also indicated, (5) though it should be noted
that a single treatment may not suffice to eradicate all such pests, because of the resistance in eggs and pupae. All books treated for insect
attack should therefore be kept under observation for at least a year,
and refumigated if necessary.

For paper which is deteriorating through the intrinsic defects of the
materials, the counsel of perfection is to have all the books completely
de-acidified by the 'Chicago process' developed by R D Smith(6) or
one of the other de-acidification processes currently being developed.
Their state of development is not yet such that libraries can buy

equipment for mechanised whole book de-acidification, with the low cost per unit that Smith's concept requires, and until such equipment is available the costs of wholesale de-acidification are far too high for it to be the routine measure one hopes it will become. For the present, the librarian is likely to rely on the control of environmental factors for those books and documents in his care whose state is not yet causing concern.

For those books whose condition is parlous, the librarian will have to choose from several possible courses of action, and in his choice he will be guided by the use which is to be made of the material in his library, by costs, and of course by the advice of his restorer. In some instances washing and resizing of the affected leaves will be enough. For books in worse state, or which will receive heavy use, the choice after de-acidification will be between silking or tissuing (together with repairing tears, replacing missing fragments, and reinforcing edges) or lamination with cellulose acetate film. Plastic lamination may be the only practicable solution for holding together fragile documents (such as newspapers) which are printed on mechanical wood papers. The use of soluble nylon for reinforcement, as developed in the British Museum Research Laboratory, would appear to offer many significant advantages in conservation work.

Whichever of these processes is adopted, the work can only be done by reducing the book to its separate leaves; this disbinding and rebinding adds alarmingly to the costs of what is already an expensive operation.

In many instances, the librarian may have to protect his materials for the future by reducing present use of them. To enclose the leaves of frequently used manuscripts (such as letters) in cellulose acetate envelopes sealed on three sides is one way of providing protection without depriving the readers of access to the original material. In other cases, eg for heavily used but highly fragile newspapers, conservation must take priority over the wish to allow readers to use original materials, and the use of microfilm copies will be indicated. There will be instances in which the microfilm will not be a satisfactory substitute, of course, and in such it will be within the librarian's discretion to permit the use of the original. But the provision of microfilms, or the

Plate 3: A small conservation department at work: the Jamaica Archives. The craftsman in the foreground is silking a decayed manuscript; in the background restored leaves are being resown for binding.

use of full-size offset litho reprints when they exist, will greatly en-hance the life of the originals.

On occasion, the librarian will have in his care materials which are in too bad a state to be made available to readers at all, until they have been repaired, and the backlog of work that the conservation depart-ments attached to record offices (for example) may have, could mean that it will be years before the material is available to readers. Natur-ally one tries to avoid this sort of situation, but the publicity which may surround the deposit of a collection like a parish library in the rare book room will at times produce enquiries for the use of material which is not in a fit state for presentation. The professional scholar will understand why, but others may not, and some very unwelcome publicity can result from having material not available for con-sultation.

Cleaning

As well as inspecting his new stock for signs of deterioration, the rare books librarian has to see that the materials coming under his care are clean. Cleanliness is the chief guard against the rapid deterioration of books, but there is little point in endeavouring to create the right environmental conditions, with proper air filtration and so forth, if one allows the books to come into the library dirty. There is dirt and dirt, and most books purchased from usual trade sources as rare book prices will be clean indeed compared with the offerings of a deceased scholar's attic. But all should be cleaned with a small hand vacuum cleaner with soft bristles round the nozzle; inside and out. No more than this may be required for many books before they go into the collection.

In other cases, cleaning according to a recognised procedure(7) will be indicated. There are those who will lament the loss of a book's 'old' look, but the patina of age is a quite different thing from dirt and neglect; in any case, the preservation of bindings through treatment with British Museum leather dressing or some similar formula demands the cleaning of the binding prior to treatment. For dealing with the occasional complaint that one is destroying a book's patina the present writer has found it useful to keep an early eighteenth century book to hand, one volume of which had been washed and treated with leather dressing and the other volume left in its original grubby and untreated state. Some institutions, such as the Jamaica Archives, keep a small display case of 'before and after' specimens as an object lesson for those who doubt the importance of conservation and cleaning measures.

The organisation of conservation and restoration work
Some elementary conservation work, such as the cleaning and dressing of bindings alluded to above, can be undertaken in any library, however small, by the staff of the special collection. In most instances it is to be assumed that the rare book collection forms only a part of a larger library, and that its needs for conservation and restoration measures will have to be fitted into the institution's normal administrative pattern for binding and repair work. If the library has its own bindery, the master binder at least should have had training in restoration work, and some of the rare book collection's needs can be entrusted to him for his personal attention.

If the operation is large enough, the bindery will include such special equipment as fumigation chambers and laminators, and more of the work needed by the rare books librarian can be done in house. The ideal situation from the librarian's point of view is that in which the library is sufficiently large-scale for its staff to include a conservation expert full-time, as well as other binding staff able to work competently under his direction.

When the library is not large enough for this, it is sometimes possible to secure the part-time services of an authority on conservation, on a consultancy basis. If the library lacks any bindery, one has of course to go outside for all the necessary restoration work, which by no means all binders are equipped to undertake. The advice of other rare book librarians and of archivists should be sought in such cases, since more binders may proclaim themselves able to undertake work than should be entrusted with it.

Even when the library does have its own bindery, and a master binder sympathetic to the peculiar needs of the special collection, the rare books librarian should be able to go outside for specialist work when it seems necessary. To go to an outside expert is naturally likely to be more costly, and in the short term may be difficult to justify except for the high-spots of the collection, but in the long term to get the best attention possible will be an economy.

References

1 At the very least the librarian will know the Library Association's research publication no 10 *The care of books and documents* London, 1973. Most librarians seriously concerned with conservation problems will at least scan the issues of *Restaurator: international journal for the preservation of library and archival material*, published in Copenhagen by Restaurator Press since 1969.

2 Quoted from a paper on the principles of archive repair, given by Roger Ellis at the opening of the first course in record repair at the London School of Printing, 1951.

3 To attend a binding course which is not specifically concerned with restoration can be very instructive in opening one's eyes to trade binding practices which are anything but desirable from the conservationist's point of view.

4 I am told that Latin American dealers will immerse books attacked by mould in petrol: a method whose long term effects one does not like to think about.

5 Deep freezing for a short period is an attractive alternative for collections too small to justify the acquisition of fumigation equipment. The writer has found the use of an ordinary domestic freezer perfectly satisfactory for this purpose.

6 R D Smith 'New approaches to preservation' in *Library quarterly* vol 40 no 1, January 1970, pp 139–75.

7 Such as those recommended in Carolyn Horton's *Cleaning and preserving bindings* or Bernard Middleton's *Restoration of leather bindings*.

Chapter VII
The housing of special collections

From the point of view of the previous chapter, that of concern for the conservation of the material housed in a rare book collection, one can formulate a number of guiding principles to be followed in planning the physical accommodation and furnishings of the collection. This aspect of housing the collections is one which is considered below. Other factors are also relevant for consideration, including the premises desirable for use of the collection's materials; increasingly security for collections which command a high monetary value is a problem which exercises the minds of curators.

It is scarcely necessary to indicate that the comments which follow have been prepared in the belief that the special collection comprises the books and other graphic materials in the library, and not the furnishings or equipment of the library. There are of course instances in which the library itself, in its building or furniture, is a sort of bibliographical coelocanth. The chained books at Wimborne Minster, Chetham's Library at Manchester, the Pepysian Library at Cambridge—indeed many of the collections described so well in Anthony Hobson's *Great libraries*—are important as examples of library architecture or library planning of different periods or kinds, as much as they are for the books they contain. When one is concerned with the maintenance of collections housed in buildings or shelving of historic importance—where the libraries are themselves a kind of museum-piece—naturally very different considerations will apply from those postulated below. However convinced of the virtues of fluorescent tube lighting, say, one would scarcely advocate its introduction into Coimbra University Library!

Even for modern foundations, there will frequently be instances in which aesthetic considerations will have to take precedence over some of the points discussed in this chapter. The architectural conceptions embodied in, say, the John Rylands Library, the Hunt Botanical

Library or the Folger Shakespeare Library—to take three twentieth century libraries, housed in buildings designed for them—will impose many constraints on the equipment employed in the housing and use of the books kept in these libraries.

Buildings

It is unusual indeed for the rare books librarian to enjoy the privilege of working cooperatively with an architect in the design of a building intended specifically and solely for the special collections. Much more usually, even in the case of new premises, the rare book room will form only a part of a much larger complex, and its special needs will have to be fitted in to the general pattern, if they can be fitted in at all. In preparing a brief for an architect, several considerations will apply. Physical security for the rare books will require that the department is outside areas of heavy traffic, though with easy access from it to areas of general reference and bibliography. Security will also require that the department be situated close to those other service departments (such as binding or photography) which are frequently called upon to meet its needs. An exhibition area and lecture hall are very desirable adjacent to the rare books department rather than within its quarters.

The collections coming within the control of the department will include the rare materials themselves, and a range of secondary reference works (bibliographies, for example) which will be required for readers to use in conjunction with the rare books.(1) This secondary material, or a substantial proportion of the more commonly used part of it, may advantageously be shelved on open access within the department's reading room, as is done so well, for example, in the rare book room of the Bibliothèque Royale in Brussels.

The rare books themselves however will be housed under conditions of much stricter security, in stacks to which direct reader access, though seldom completely prohibited,(2) will be the exception rather than the rule.

This limitation of direct access to the research materials increases security not only from the aspect of theft or mutilation or rough handling, but also as regards conservation. Books tend to survive better in conditions of subdued light or no light at all, and at temperatures rather lower than those comfortable for humans. These measures can be achieved in a closed stack in a way that is impossible for an open access collection.

Lighting
Direct sunlight is always bad for books, and it is important that all stock, whether open or closed access, should be screened from direct sunlight and that the exposure to artificial light be limited as far as possible.

Recommendations for lighting standards have increased very considerably in the past half century. In 1932, for instance, ten footcandles was recommended as a minimal level for reading rooms; by the mid-fifties the level recommended had risen to between thirty to fifty footcandles, and in the libraries of today intensities of seventy to one hundred footcandles are not unknown.

In addition to the greater intensity of lighting, its quality has changed. The widespread replacement of incandescent lighting by fluorescent, even when the latter is adequately filtered, tends to increase the damaging effects of radiation (although, to be just, one must record that carefully chosen fluorescent lighting is not significantly worse than similarly screened incandescent lamps, and will be better than unscreened lighting of the latter type).

These changes present problems in the planning of rare book collections. 'Increasing values of illumination bring with them increasing probabilities of deterioration'(3) and the librarian has to reconcile the demands his readers will reasonably make for lighting not significantly worse than they will be used to, or find in other areas of the library, with his conservation requirements. Subdued lighting is easily achieved in stack and other shelving areas; in reading rooms subdued general lighting will be acceptable if greater intensities can be obtained by the individual reader by means of desk lights.

Heating and environmental control
Low temperatures will not damage bookstock and may increase its life, but even in closed access stack areas in which reader comfort is not a matter of concern methods of temperature control are needed, in

cool temperate climates as in warmer areas. Heating cannot however be considered in isolation, since without other control methods changes in temperature will bring with them changes in humidity, often in such a way that different areas of the library will have very different microclimates. In one part of the library it is possible for condensation from cold outer windows to subject material there to undesirably damp conditions, while a few feet away radiators or hot air ducts may be baking the life out of the stock. Particularly when books are stored in closed cases it is possible for extremely undesirable microclimatic conditions to exist.

To reduce these variations in microclimate as far as possible a good air circulatory system is necessary. This demands heating, ventilation, air filtration, cooling and humidity control installations; all operating within narrow limits in order to maintain conditions close to the ideal, regardless of the conditions prevailing outside the library. Humidity control is probably the most important factor in this respect, to inhibit microbiological activity on the one hand, and to prevent desiccation of paper and binding materials on the other. Temperature control alone cannot do this: low temperature storage will not prevent the growth of moulds, as witness any domestic refrigerator in which things have been stored too long.

In many instances control of temperature and humidity alone will go a considerable way to providing an acceptable storage climate. But this will not offer any protection against atmospheric pollutants, which are a serious problem not only in large industrial centres, but also in areas one might not anticipate. The Archives in Georgetown, Guyana, for example, are so housed that their atmosphere carries not only sea breezes (which play havoc through the corrosion of steel shelving) but also at times heavy pollution from the exhaust fumes of passing traffic. Air filtration, through a properly operated airconditioning system, not only reduces such pollution to a much more acceptable level but also (by creating a closed atmosphere) helps to prevent macrobiological attack on the contents of the library.

The value of airconditioning from this point of view is well understood by librarians who work in climates subject to the sort of

97

attack described by W J Plumbe in his *Preservation of books in tropical and subtropical countries* (Kuala Lumpur, OUP, 1964). As an instance of its effectiveness in removing acidic pollutants a table given in a paper by R E Waller(4) is very instructive.

Despite the evident advantages of air conditioning there will be cases in which the librarian cannot secure it, particularly in small special collections housed in older buildings. In these cases, though long-term protection may be impossible, the librarian can nevertheless take steps to see, for example, that the shelving of his stock is so planned that gusts of hot dry air are not being blown directly on to the books by the heating system, and that (in heated buildings) humidity levels are not dropping too low. At the most primitive level, even having dishes of water in the worst areas can be of help!

Fire protection
If the special collection is housed in a modern building of fireproof construction, the direct danger of destruction from fire is relatively slight, though some small libraries in historic buildings are potentially in a very hazardous situation. The greatest danger in the modern building comes from the preventive measures against fire, at least when these rely on automatic sprinkler systems for fire protection: save when a fire completely consumes the building the damage caused to the stock by water is generally far greater than that caused by the heat and flames.

When local ordinances require the provision of standpipes in public areas of the buildings, fogmaking devices are far preferable to spraynozzles, being equally effective and much less destructive to books. Foam extinguishers, used in conjunction with an automatic fire detection system, are efficient in putting the fire out with minimal moisture damage to the stock.

In those rare book collections which are not in buildings of fireproof construction, dry-type extinguishers (of the kind emitting methyl bromide, carbon tetrachloride or carbon dioxide) will be necessary equipment in each room; strategically placed asbestos blankets can also be of considerable help in reducing damage.

Security

During the hours that the library is open, theft and vandalism will be controlled by adequate reading-room supervision and by the check-out measures described in chapter VIII. During the hours that the library is closed, measures of the kind appropriate for museums' collections will be required. These will be particularly important for material displayed in the library's exhibition areas, and for the high-spots of the collection, for which last special vaults within the stack may be appropriate. The advice of the local police should be sought in deciding what security measures, alarm devices and so forth should be used. In my experience their proposals will often go further than is practicable for a library to adopt—one cannot turn the rare book room into a Fort Knox—but will nevertheless be very helpful to the librarian, while the police may also appreciate knowing that there is a potential target of theft in a place that they would not anticipate. Just as the police should be consulted, so the advice of the company with which the collection is insured should be sought.

Shelving and storage

The more valuable parts of the research collection will be shelved in closed access situations, and therefore (it is to be presumed) out of public vision. For this reason, one's concern with the physical housing can be concentrated upon the suitability of the shelving and other storage equipment from the conservation aspect, and consideration of the equipment from the interior decorator's point of view will be of concern only for the public areas. To be sure, there are design considerations to be born in mind when installing stack shelving, but these will be practical rather than aesthetic. It goes without saying that the intervals between shelves must be such that the top edges of books are not bruised when they are removed or replaced, that shelf ends and book supports must be of such a design that books cannot be damaged on them, and that the shelf depth must be sufficient to prevent any volumes from projecting beyond the lip of the shelf.

A substantial proportion of material will be too slim or fragile for shelving directly. If the collection contains fine bindings, for example, one would not shelve them without protection. To reduce wear and

Plate 4: Record storage in a tropical climate: the Jamaica Archives. Note the horizontal storage of unbound materials in document boxes, and the use of economical shelving in a closed-access area.

tear these will be boxed, as of course will pamphlet and some manuscript material.

The design and construction of these boxes, to be consistent with the needs of conservation, requires that they be made of good quality acid-free materials, so that they cannot contaminate their contents. Boxes with removable lids or fall-down covers are to be preferred to those of the traditional solander box or slipcase type, since the removal of books from the latter subjects the spines to strain and the sides to abrasion. (6) Such boxes are best stored flat in stacks of two or three on the shelves, rather than standing upright, since the contents can easily be bent and damaged when too few are in a box which is kept standing.

Manuscript material presents a number of different problems. Some single-leaf manuscripts may be kept in cellulose acetate envelopes. All should be kept unfolded, in sturdy acid-free filecovers or envelopes, and for preference stored in document boxes kept flat, like those used for pamphlet material. They are sometimes kept stored in vertical files, which is considerably more convenient for access when there are large numbers to deal with, but whether in the older filing cabinets or in lateral files such methods are far less satisfactory because of the risk that the flimsy document will get tattered or crumpled at the bottom of the file, and because of the much greater chance of damage at removal or replacement than is the case when boxes are used.

Reading room furnishing

In the rare book department's public areas, the shelving that will be used for housing the bibliographies and other reference books used in conjunction with the rare material will be of normal library type. The allocation of space in the reading areas can advantageously be rather more generous than in other departments of the library. Some at least of the reading tables should be oversize, and desirably all should have enough aisle space alongside for a trolley to hold the reader's books. A reader consulting three or four large folios plus ancillary aids and his own notes will run out of table space very quickly. The provision of larger tables and trolleys for such occasions is not merely a courtesy easing the reader's use of the books, it is a precaution against damage to them.

A similar precaution is in the provision of lecterns, since if they are used there is much less risk of readers resting other material they are consulting on the rare books which have been issued to them. Sometimes these lecterns are built into the reading desks, but it is generally a better policy to have separate lecterns which can be provided as necessary, since the kind which is built in creates a rather inflexible working surface, and can be a thorough nuisance to the reader who is consulting, let us say, duodecimos printed in a very small type size.

The reading tables or desks should be provided with individual lights, so that those readers who need higher candlepower for particular types of material can have it without an overall higher intensity of lighting. Because a good deal of the research undertaken in special collections is fairly long term, it is desirable that readers should be able to keep some of their own materials on the premises from day to day. For reasons of supervision and security it is not very practicable to have carrels; to have reading tables provided with lockable drawers, and which readers can book for their regular use, is a way of approaching this problem. Another, rather less satisfactory, is to provide lockers.

The only normal exceptions to the statement about carrels, given above, will be in those instances that readers need to use typewriters, tape-recorders and other similar aids either of their own, or provided by the library. The use of equipment of this kind clearly calls for special accommodation with sound baffles to prevent interference for other readers. Similarly special areas will be needed for those who need to consult microtexts, compare editions in a collating machine, inspect watermarks and so forth. It is important to remember, in planning these areas, that their users are going to need just as much room as other readers in addition to the space occupied by the special equipment they are using: the poor wretch doing research with microfilm is sufficiently handicapped by just that, without having insufficient desk space for his other books as well!

Plate 5: The reading room of the Réserve Precieuse, Bibliothèque Royale Albert 1er, Brussels. Note the portable lecterns and the open-access shelving of reference material.

Special equipment

All special collections are likely to include some, and perhaps a substantial proportion of their materials in microtext. In many cases microfilm copies of fragile materials will be the form normally made available to readers; even though the library holds the originals, conservation requirements will demand the use of the substitute whenever possible.

There is a wide range of readers for microforms on the market, with varying virtues, but few of them are designed on ergonomic principles. What the reader requires is an image of sufficient intensity and clarity for him to consult, and copy from, without strain; and this perhaps for periods of many hours at a stretch. To have to keep looking up at a screen and then down to one's paper, or to have to adjust the controls constantly to get the full page on to the screen is horrible and unnecessary, though imposed on the user by many machines. The ideal, I would suggest, is a reader capable of variable focus(7) and of different intensities of lighting, which has simple and easily accessible controls for insertion of the microforms, for winding on and other adjustments. If such a reader exists at a reasonable price I have yet to have the pleasure of using it! Because of the drawbacks of most of the machines currently available, the library should have several of different types—including a reader-printer so that the library user may be spared some of the misery of using microtexts in their original form.

For some types of research work, a collating machine will be necessary. These are several interesting accounts of the construction of such machines,(8) and for the moderately sized collection in which some work of this kind is required the adaptation of a pair of microfilm readers would appear a practicable and relatively cheap proposition.

There will be occasions on which readers may legitimately need other aids. Some documents indecipherable by natural light may give up their secrets when viewed in ultra-violet light, for instance. To be able to inspect the watermarks in a book's paper is a necessary part of some types of research. For the reader to have to hold a book with fragile leaves up to the light is a sure way of arousing alarm in the reading room superintendant, who will correctly regard such proceedings with disfavour. The provision or improvisation of a light-table will make such lines of research simpler and more efficient, and far less damaging to the materials. Such aids as these cannot of course form part of the equipment of the reading room, but may be provided in the library's photographic unit, which will normally be concerned more closely with such work.

Exhibition equipment

To mount exhibitions is not normally the raison d'être of a rare book collection, though it may contribute powerfully to their work. When the collection is a department of a larger library, the exhibition areas may be outside the control of the rare book librarian, though one hopes they will be within his sphere of influence.

It is very important that the display cases to be used meet the requirements necessary for the rare books which will from time to time be shown in them. Modern display cases (the Varedplan cases, for instance) if capable of being locked securely and of being monitored by a theft detection system will normally be satisfactory. The microclimate of the case is an important consideration also; if the cases have lighting installed it must be of a type which will not be deleterious to the materials on display eg filtered warm-white fluorescent tubes.

In addition to the display cases for books, there will be need in many cases for wall display equipment for prints, broadsides and the like, and for some of the interchangeable panel type display boards (eg Marler-Haley) to be used for the background material to the exhibitions.

References

1 Some of the reference material required by readers in the rare book reading room will not normally be housed there, of course, but will have to be transferred there from other parts of the library as the need arises.

2 Many users of special collections will, when they have sufficiently cogent reasons, be permitted to undertake searches in the stack (perhaps under direct supervision) to obviate time-wasting searches through the catalogues which might be quite inadequate for the purpose. Being locked in the stacks of the Newberry for a couple of

hours enabled the writer to pin-point the half dozen or so pamphlet boxes of manuscript and ephemeral material he needed for research on a certain private press, whereas if limited to the use of the catalogues he would have had to request perhaps twenty times that number to cover his needs. Similarly, without direct access to certain areas of the stacks of the Bodleian the research underlying Geoffrey Wakeman's *Victorian book illustration* Newton Abbot, David & Charles, 1973 would not have been possible.

3 Carl Wessel, 'Environmental factors affecting the permanence of library materials' *Library quarterly* vol 40 no 1, Jan 1970, pp 39–84. This discusses in detail, and with copious references, the problems of lighting and the other elements in environmental control.

4 'Studies on the nature of urban air pollution' in *Museum climatology* ed by G Thompson, London, International Institute of Conservation, 1967.

5 *Museum* vol 17 (1964) includes a report prepared by Interpol at the request of the International Council on Museums, which analyses the problems and gives plans for defensive and detective methods of control.

6 Specifications for boxes for the US National Archives are given in the *American archivist* vol 13 (1950) pp 233–6, and vol 17 (1954) pp 237–42.

7 At times, particularly with manuscripts in difficult hands, it is helpful to have an image larger than the original; for other purposes one smaller than the original will permit quicker scanning, while on other occasions an image the exact size of the original is needed.

8 Such machines are described in Richard Levin, 'A poor man's collating machine' *Research opportunities in renaissance drama* vol 9, (1966) pp 25–6; Vinton A Dearing 'The poor man's Mark IV or ersatz Hinman collator' *Papers of the Bibliographical Society of America* vol 60, (1966) pp 149–58; and Gerald A Smith. 'Collating machine, poor man's, Mark VII' *Papers of the Bibliographical Society of America* vol 61 (1967) pp 110–13.

Chapter VIII
Organisation of collections for use, I

There is a dichotomy in the organisation of rare book collections for use. On the one hand the librarian, guided by his role as conservator, is concerned to devise methods of control over the use of the materials in his care, hedging them around with various restrictions so that they will survive for the enjoyment of posterity even if at the inconvenience of present users. On the other hand, organisation for use involves a very positive and outgoing public relations attitude to the collections, intended to make their resources better known and better utilized for general cultural purposes at a popular level as well as for scholarly research.

This chapter is concerned with those aspects of work in special collections which are essentially pasive, and concerned with giving service to those readers and other users of the collection who request it. These will include the serious reader undertaking genuine research, who knows with some precision what he wants, and how his needs can best be served from that collection. It will also include the reader (perhaps equally serious) whose ideas of his needs are less clear-cut and who may in fact be served best elsewhere. There will be the casual visitors, whose purpose in visiting the collection is not for research at all, but who are visiting the library as they would a museum, and want to see something of its treasures. These are naturally commoner in famous libraries, but delegates at conferences and other visitors to universities (for example) may frequently be brought to the rare books room because it is here that the individuality of the library best shows itself.

In addition, there will be postal enquiries, which may outnumber the direct personal visits, and which will vary from the exactly worded and highly sophisticated query whose answer will involve very considerable research, to the vague general request from somebody whose needs can be met very simply from other sources.

Control of use

For purposes of conservation the use of rare books has to be restricted to those who really need them. The security policies which rare book librarians have to enforce if they are to perform their function as conservators can cause resistance and hostility when the reasons for them are not understood. When a library is tax-supported, it is particularly difficult to avoid the danger of alienating those whose feeling is that their tax deductions may be considered as supporting the library. Nevertheless, in practice nearly all rare book librarians will impose some restrictions on the use of the collections.

The restrictions will vary considerably. In large rare book libraries which are heavily used, intending readers are advised to write in advance, stating the research they intend to undertake in the collections, and they may be required to give references before an admission ticket is granted (and the references may be taken up). In some institutions a letter of application is not sufficient, applicants for tickets being required to fill out a lengthy questionnaire. In universities the use of the special collections may be limited to academic staff and graduate research students (who may be required to present a letter of recommendation from their thesis supervisor) plus specially admitted outside readers.

Even in less formalised situations, a member of the staff of the rare book room will usually interview the intending reader, partly in order to ascertain his needs and therefore to be able to cater to them better, but also partly to be able to guide away those enquirers whose needs can be as well supplied by the use of reprints or other materials housed in other collections.(1)

This vetting of intending readers is not something which is resented by the readers unless very crudely done. The pertinacious enquirer, even sans letters of recommendation, will generally be admitted to the use of the collections, and may well not realise that the friendly conversation he has had with the librarian was an interview testing his bona fides.

Nor will the reader normally resent the stringent rules which are needed for the use of the materials in the collection, provided they are explained to him. These will include the security precaution that all coats, attaché cases etc are deposited in the cloakroom and not brought into the reading room. They will require that the reader handles with care the books issued to him: not resting his own papers, notes or other books on them, nor (for example) placing his fingers on the illuminated areas of manuscripts. For tightly bound volumes the library may provide means of holding the leaves open (eg a glass plate) and require that it be used. Tracing and photography, unless prior permission has been given, will not be allowed.

In many instances, libraries will require that readers use only pencils for note-taking, pens of all descriptions being forbidden. With the development of ballpens and fibretips some libraries have relaxed this requirement, banning only the use of ink pens (and even fountain pens are less frowned upon than at one time). I am not sure whether this relaxation of the older rules is altogether wise: the damage that can be done by a reader whose ballpoint ink has got on to his fingers is not much less than that caused by a leaking fountain pen.

A special problem is at times presented by readers' need to consult volumes in the collection which have unopened leaves (that is, with the bolts at head and foredge still uncut). In such cases, the library staff will insist they open the leaves; a task calling for more care than readers can safely be expected to give.

The reading room staff will of course keep careful surveillance over the use being made of the books in the library. When a new reader first uses the collection, it is the course of prudence to look with a careful eye at the way he handles the books which are issued to him. This can be done with discretion, and a moment or two will be enough to show whether he is a bookman familiar with handling rare books or not. Even the experienced bookmen may be wrong'uns—and in every rare book librarian's mind is the image of T J Wise sitting in the North Library of the British Museum, calmly tearing leaves out of the pre-restoration dramatists—but if a reader's handling of the books indicates that he knows the rules, surveillance of his use of the books will naturally be lessened.

In some instances, special guidance can with advantage be given to the reader at the time his books are issued to him. If a particular volume is in a very frail binding, or its paper in an advanced state of decay, for the librarian to warn the reader to take special care in consulting the book is wise; and such advice will be taken as a courtesy by the reader. A good many readers will in any case have a considerable respect for the books they are using, and will appreciate being shown the safest way to turn the leaves in a fragile volume.

To give this guidance is a simple matter in a small collection with a small number of users at any one time. In a larger library (in which, for instance, books will be brought to readers by attendants rather than by the professional library staff) it is a less easy matter. However, even in such cases it is possible to provide a printed notice which will accompany the book, indicating its fragile state and warning that care must be exercised in its use.

Issue methods
It is normal practice in rare book collections for the readers to be required to complete a requisition slip for any of the rare books kept in closed access which they wish to use (and also for any materials which are being transferred from other departments for their use in the rare book room) although the reference material on the open shelves can be consulted without formality.

These requisition slips are generally in duplicate, of self-carboning stock, and demand the basic bibliographic details (author, title, date), the shelf-mark, reader's name, ticket and seat numbers and the date of issue. Some libraries restrict the number of volumes which can be issued at one time to a reader, and will accept no more than six requisitions at one time. This is not a very helpful rule: readers are not often going to undertake the chore of filling in requisition slips for books they do not need, and when there is a long delay in books being fetched from the stacks for readers (a notorious cause for complaint in some rare book collections) its imposition can result in needless frustration and waste of time.(2)

When the book is fetched from the stacks, one copy of the requisition slip is placed in a holder on the shelves in the place of the volume being removed; the second copy forms the loan record which is kept at the desk until the book is returned after use by the reader, when he receives it back as a receipt for the return. The slip on the shelves will remain there until the book is reshelved, when the slips will be filed as a record of use.

It is normal, even when a reader intends using material over an extended period, to require its return to the desk for discharging at the end of each day, although for convenience books will be kept there (and not returned to the shelves) for the reader to reclaim them the next day. (3.)

The volume of loans in a rare book collection is not such as to make so simple a system impracticable. Some libraries do not permanently file the duplicate slips removed from the shelves when the books are reshelved, but the fact that readers *know* that a library retains a permanent record of loans acts as a disincentive to those who might otherwise be tempted to remove plates or cause other damage. And such a record can be of real value at times (in cases of theft, misplaced books and so forth) since it provides an accurate record that the book was still in place on a certain date. Sometimes there are other benefits of a less obvious sort: the British Museum's loan slips filled in by Karl Marx are scarcely without interest . . .

Assistance to readers
Since the rarer parts of the collection will not be available to readers on open access—save in the unusual instances that the readers are permitted into the stacks, which will of course be subject to rather stringent security precautions—the readers' reliance on the catalogues and on the help of the staff will be greater than in some other types of library work. Not infrequently the reader may be seeking certain printed books or manuscripts for which his information, culled from a bibliography or a citation, may be in a form which does not make for easy identification in the catalogues, even although he knows the library possesses the work.(4) Assistance to readers will be even more important in special collections since, from the nature of the collection, the catalogue entries may be under headings which differ from the normal.

In a pungent and memorable letter in the *Library Association record* Veronica Barker recently wrote of 'the provision of a sham information service which is actually a minor pastime of unqualified staff at an issue desk.' However true this may be of libraries in general it certainly must not be true of the research collection which by its very nature purports to offer a higher level of service than can prevail in more general collections. Since new readers will be interviewed by a senior member of staff as a matter of routine, one of the basic problems encountered in libraries—of getting the readers to ask their questions of the right person—should not arise, provided that senior staff are always on duty in the reading room, as they should be. The senior staff will be qualified in at least some of the fields covered by the collection, and experienced in others, and in many cases themselves involved in practical research.

Sometimes, since the kind of enquiry received can be pretty esoteric, the reader will not so much seek guidance as be able to give it. It is by no means unusual for rare book librarians to seek the assistance of visiting scholars on certain points, or at any rate to compare notes with them. This is of course flattering to the reader, and will tend to put him on a different and much less formal relationship with the library staff. The ideal situation, one which really can exist on a gratifyingly large number of occasions, is when there can be a useful interchange of information; when librarian and reader realise that they are members of the same invisible college.

One category of visitor, already referred to, is the casual visitor who is to be shown something of the collections. If there is an exhibition area, such guided visits will naturally centre around the material on show, with other books being brought out as seems requisite. The range of visitors is very wide, from groups of schoolchildren through parties of library school students and others, to the individual book collector, librarian or scholar working in related areas, who may be taking advantage of a visit to the vicinity to undertake reconnaisance with research use of the library possibly to follow later.

This public relations aspect of the rare books librarian's work will normally include a short talk on the history of the library and its collections, geared of course to the needs of the visitors and the time available. Naturally one will expect that group visits will be prearranged, so that the librarian can prepare some of the books to be shown, and one will prefer it if the individual has also made an appointment. But the librarian will often have to receive such visitors at short notice, and may have to play it by ear in deciding what sort of tour to give the visitor.(5)

Postal enquiries

A large number of the enquiries calling for reference service will be received by post, or less frequently by telephone. Naturally enough any potential user of the library who has to invest time and travel in visiting the library will wish to assure himself beforehand that he will be able to find the materials and services he needs. General enquiries of this kind can to some extent be answered by a form letter, accompanied by a booklet on the nature and range of the research collections, like the excellent pamphlet *Opportunities for research at the John Carter Brown Library*. But they will generally call for a limited literature search as well. Other enquiries may call for any number of bibliographical matters—whether the library has a certain book, whether its copy has a certain provenance, whether it is in its original binding, whether it has certain advertisement leaves, what is its format, how its paper is watermarked and so forth. The librarian ought to be able, as a matter of routine, to deal with any of the simpler enquiries which will come in this way: to be able to state how a book is gathered, for example. One hesitates to say that the librarian should be able to answer questions on all the points dealt with in Gaskell's *New introduction to bibliography*—I for one would be very unhappy to have it regarded as my duty to identify a particular typeface—but I ought to have enough understanding of the problems to supply the reader with enough information (including a photocopy of a suitable page) to enable him to make the identification. Some indication that librarians are less efficient in this than they should be is given by John Hetherington in his article 'Signatures and sizes'.(6)

As a frequent user of rare book collections at long distance, I have been impressed with the care that some libraries devote to the most vaguely worded enquiry. A letter to the Bancroft Library at Berkeley, asking what early Belizean imprints they possessed, produced a prompt description of several items unique to that library, plus references to others which they did not possess but which the librarian had tracked down in *NUC pre-1956 imprints*. Since there is no chance, when faced with a letter, of asking the enquirer for further details, librarians in many special collections make it their practice to give supplementary information as well as that asked for. Writing to the librarian of Rhodes House Library to ask about their holdings of the first Belize newspaper, I received not only the details I had requested, but also the information that their copies had belonged to a certain resident of Belize, and bore some manuscript notes which he had written, and which were quoted in the reply—and the information these contained was crucial in completing my research. Oxford libraries understand postal enquiry work and undertake it very seriously: a recent letter to the Bodleian, asking for details of the printers' imprints on three early Jamaican publications which a Jamaican bibliography stated the Bodleian possessed, produced a reply which included not only these details, but also xeroxes of the titlepages of each, *and* xeroxes of the titlepages of another dozen or so pieces of early Jamaican printing in Bodley, with Bodley's pressmarks and the references to the appropriate entries in the Jamaican bibliography added in each case. Could any reader ask for more?

Library generated research

As well as the enquiry work which will be undertaken in response to readers' enquiries or those received by post, the rare books librarian has a responsibility to scholarship at large to undertake some research even when requests for it have not been directed at his library. The bibliographical queries included as a regular feature in the *Book collector* and *Bibliography newsletter*, or the 'Information wanted' section in the *Times literary supplement* are areas in which as a matter of routine the rare books librarian should examine his stock to see whether it will be helpful in providing answers to the queries.

In many instances, too, such enquiry work may be inspired by the publication of articles and books on subjects with which the library is concerned. For example, William E Fredeman's account of 'Emily Faithfull and the Victoria Press' in the June 1974 issue of

The library included a tentative short-title catalogue of the Victoria Press's publications. Time from other responsibilities permitting, the librarian in charge of a special collection likely to contain such material has a clear duty to communicate the information to the author. In some cases the librarian will turn up sufficient fresh information to justify writing a bibliographical note for publication in an appropriate journal.

Photocopying services

To provide readers with microfilms, photographs or electrostatic prints will often form a considerable part of the work undertaken in a rare book collection.

This work has the not inconsiderable advantage of reducing the use, and hence the wear and tear, of the materials in the collection. However, since the copying processes themselves are very powerful contributors to this wear and tear, they can be provided only under very strictly controlled conditions. It is a good general rule that photography of books in the collections can only be undertaken by the library's own photographic unit or when prior permission has been granted to approved outside photographers. The larger libraries, with their own photographic laboratories, will have a regular scale of fees for the use of these laboratories by outside photographers, who will be allowed their use only under supervision. Anybody who has seen what a photographer who wants a shot of a double-spread can do to a tight binding to get it to open flat will understand the reason for this precaution!

Another rule imposed by many libraries controls the use to be made of any photographs or copies made in or provided by the library. Even when the material itself is out of copyright, a usual limitation is that the copies are provided for private study and research only, and that special permission has to be sought if the photographs are required for reproduction purposes. In many instances this is freely given, on the understanding that appropriate credits will also be printed. In other cases the library will charge a fee for the use of photographs of its materials for publication purposes, and this is certainly justified when the purpose is commercial. For photographs required by advertising

agencies, or by an offset litho reprinting house it is perfectly proper for the library to require payment, perhaps on a royalty basis, even if its normal practice is to grant permission freely for scholarly or semi-scholarly publication purposes.

The extent to which the library is under an obligation to provide photocopies or microfilms of its materials is a debatable point. On the one hand there will be the wish to provide assistance to scholars wherever they may be. On the other hand when a library has paid large sums to purchase certain important manuscripts, or the librarian has invested a lot of time and effort in persuading a benefactor to present such materials to the collection, there is often the feeling that extensive use of the materials should be reserved for the library's own readers.

One of the strongest arguments that the rare books librarian in a university can advance, when seeking funds for purchases, is that their addition to the stock will attract scholars to the university, and that their research (and that of the school of research students which will develop), perhaps to be published by the university's own press, will contribute to the academic standing of the institution. In other, cruder words, that having these books will allow the university to rise in the academic pecking order. If a library having purchased the books then distributes microfilms or other copies on a wide scale, the prestigious publication which exploits the full research value of the materials may well be published elsewhere by a scholar who has worked elsewhere: undoubtedly in the interests of scholarship, but of little use to the library which paid the bills. This is not a very attractive argument, but one can see that it has force, particularly for the relatively new institution which is struggling to build up its own research potential.

In some cases, therefore, the rare book librarian may feel that extensive requests for microfilms or other copies are unreasonable and should not be filled. Were I, for instance, to ask the Clark Library at Los Angeles to microfilm for me the whole of their collection of Eric Gill's papers it would be (in my view) an unreasonable request, though I have no doubt that they would supply information about, or microfilm copies of, individual items in the collection. Such rules about the making of copies are naturally applied more often in the case of manuscript than printed materials, since questions of copyright in the text are also present.

In many rare book collections there is a simple general rule about xerox and other contact copying: it is forbidden. Even in the more liberal institutions such copying will be permitted only when undertaken by a member of the library staff: the risks of damage to fragile volumes in unskilled hands are too great for any other policy to be reasonable. *All* copying and other photographic work must be within the discretion of the curator of the special collection: if he believes that a tightly-bound volume on decaying paper will be damaged in copying he may prohibit any contact copying; if a document is so fragile that it will be endangered by photography, this too may be prohibited until the volume has been through the hands of the restoration staff. Readers may feel frustrated by such rules, but the absolute prohibition will seldom be invoked, and the librarian's first duty as conservator will be understood by the reader when the reason is explained to him.

References

1 The requirement of the British Museum, the Huntington and other libraries that readers state on their application forms which libraries they have already consulted serves the same purpose.

2 As an instance, the writer has recently been searching Jamaican inventories for details of the stock of 18th century printers and others in the book trade. There is no way of knowing in advance whether a particular volume's examination will take a whole morning or only ten minutes to extract whatever information is relevant—so that a restriction on the number of volumes to be issued would quite often have meant the reader's time being wasted while he was waiting for fresh volumes to be fetched from the stacks.

3 Similarly this will permit users to complete slips to reserve books in advance, so that the scholar visiting (say) the British Museum for a day's work will find the books awaiting him, instead of having to idle away half the morning while they are fetched.

4 Perhaps I have been unfortunate, but on several occasions when

vainly hunting for things in library catalogues it has only been when I have produced the entry in a bibliography that the staff have been convinced that they did in fact possess the book.

5 As such a visitor on several occasions, I have noticed with some interest how to drop the right names into the conversation at the right time can make the librarian change gear, and give a fuller tour, bringing out more books to be looked at, than·I suspect he originally intended.

6 John R Hetherington 'Signatures and sizes' *Times literary supplement* 14 Oct 1965, p 928.

Chapter IX
Organisation of
collections for use, II

In promoting the use of rare book collections, and in fostering a greater knowledge of their value and resources, a programme of exhibitions is invaluable.

Many libraries, though possessing materials of considerable interest and importance, will not themselves have the space or the display cases, or indeed the stock to mount a regular series of exhibitions. Instead they will be limited to a very small display—perhaps only a couple of cases—of material which is of outstanding interest. In many, probably the majority, of university libraries in Britain the exhibition areas will not be exclusive to the rare books department, and its collections may well only have occasional use of the display areas. And of course there are some small collections of rare books which from their geographical location may be in difficulties for the arrangement of any display of their resources.

In some large libraries, particularly in national libraries, there is a museum function which will increase the importance of exhibitions, such that their organisation will call for the employment of special staff trained in display methods. One will expect from these libraries a more sophisticated level of work as a regular feature than is possible in the smaller library where the work does not bulk so large. But for most libraries exhibitions of rare books will be of three distinct types: the regular and continuing (though changing) display of some items in the collection; the special exhibition organised from the library's own resources around a particular theme; and the special exhibition conceived on a grander scale which also draws upon the resources of other libraries for a fuller conspectus of the subject being dealt with. Though all of these have some common features, the aims and problems of each need separate consideration.

Display cases
Some of the conservation requirements in display cases have already

been discussed in Chapter VII. The cases must be of such a design that their contents are protected against heat and ultraviolet light, and that their humidity should be controlled. It goes without saying that all exhibition areas should be effectively supervised during the hours that the library is open, but the display cases should also be provided with locks that are not easily forced, and that they should have other antitheft devices incorporated in them for those instances in which particularly precious materials are being displayed.

Indeed, elaborate protection can on occasion be used as a method of heightening the visitor's consciousness of the value of the exhibit. The sense of awe one experiences in gazing on the 42-line Bible in the Gutenberg-Museum, as compared, say, with looking at the copy in the King's Library at the British Museum, comes very much from the security measures one encounters.

There are other requirements that one will have of the display cases. They should be of such a design that they can take different coloured and textured backgrounds without a lot of fuss and contrivance, be furnished with stands and display aids of various shapes and sizes so that books of different formats can be shown standing, lying flat or inclined at different angles,(1) and they must be capable of standing open while one is in the process of arranging the exhibits. To be cluching a large and valuable folio in one hand while fighting with the lid of a display case with the other is an unpleasant experience.

Several different types of display case will be needed: those for displaying prints, maps and the like; those which can take large folios, and other in which small books and pamphlets will not be swamped. Some of the modern display equipment with detachable and interchangeable panels and display boards is often used with great effect.(2)

Routine displays
If the rare book department has display cases under its control for its regular use, some of the space will be used for a continuing display of some of its highspots, the books which the casual visitor to the library will wish to see. The problems of museum items like these are many;

often there is a particular map, or plate, or passage in the text, which it is particularly appropriate should be displayed. But the deleterious effects of light are such that good housekeeping demands that the volume is *not* kept open perpetually at the same place, but that instead the accelerated decay caused by exhibition should be alleviated by the regular turning of the pages.

To have a rotating display, with some thirty or forty books regularly used for the purpose, of which only a quarter or so are on exhibition at any one time is a method of dealing with this problem of deterioration through exhibition. It is a method which offers other advantages too: regular users of the library will not be blinded by familiarity if the exhibits change. They will look at the fresh books shown, instead of passing them by, and the general cultural value of the exhibition will be enhanced by its variety. Further, since readers will from time to time need to consult items which are on display (perhaps needing them in the reading room for extended periods) a rotating display enables the library staff easily to substitute other books for those removed from the cases. (3)

Part of the routine display will often be reserved for special material. This may be new additions to the stock; it may be a small display built around a particular anniversary, the publication of a new book, the holding of a conference. One can predict safely that many American libraries will in 1976 be mounting displays about the themes of 1776; that the approaching quincentennial of Caxton's introduction of printing into England will be celebrated by many small exhibitions as well as those organised nationally. The variety of possible themes is endless; the purpose of course is to choose material from the collections to illustrate in some way the resources of the library, and to indicate some of the research uses of this material. To this end, occasional deliberately eccentric themes and selection can have a very real value.

Even for these small regular displays, which will not be publicized widely nor mounted for any length of time, the same care in presentation will be necessary as for the special exhibition. The books to be displayed must in every instance be accompanied by a note explaining what is exhibited, and why. It should always be possible for the visitor looking at the books on display to identify them adequately (to

121

have author, title, date and shelfmark) and from the annotation to gather the significance of the particular item in relation to the overall theme of the display. To be able to state succinctly, and in an interesting way, why a particular item is on show is by no means easy, but it is the essence of these exhibition notes.

A record will of course be kept in the library of the items which are currently on display, together with copies of the exhibition notes. These exhibition notes for items used for the regular rotating displays will naturally be filed ready for use in the future; so should the notes prepared for the special displays, since the research which went into their preparation may often be of use subsequently for reference purposes. It is by no means unusual for readers to enquire later, often considerably later, about particular items which they have seen displayed and which they now wish to consult for a particular line of research. And they will come armed only with the vaguest information—that it was a small book in such and such a display case about a year ago—which will defeat recall through the conventional catalogues, but may be found when these notes are retained.

Special exhibitions
Frequently the staff of a special collection, given enough time to plan ahead, will wish to go beyond the confines of the normal small diqplay. They will instead arrange an exhibition developed out of the library's own resources, whose purpose is less the basic one of catching the eye of those visiting the library than the much more ambitious programme of attracting people to come specifically for the purpose of viewing that exhibition. In the eyes of many, the standing of the library will be judged very much on the basis of such exhibitions rather than on the services provided in the reading rooms: as an exercise in public relations they can therefore be very successful—but if badly done they can be damaging to the library's standing in the community.

Very considerable research must therefore go into the preparation of such an exhibition. The first problem, of course, once a certain theme is mooted, is the bibliographical investigation to see that the library has the resources to mount such an exhibition adequately. This investigation will necessarily involve a refinement of the theme:

an exhibition if it is to be worth the name is more than the display of some of the library's books on a certain subject. There must be a distinct pattern, or series of patterns intertwining like the plot and sub-plots of a Victorian novel, so that the visitor to the exhibition gains some coherently organised information, and is not left with a confused jumble of ill-related snippets.

To be sure, in many cases the nature of the subject and the books upon it will predetermine the classification which underlies the arrangement of the exhibition. But even for a limited subject a number of different arrangements will be possible. An exhibition on Anthony Trollope could adopt a simple chronological treatment of his career as a writer—or it could explore it in a different way by looking at the other members of his family who were writers, by grouping his works into the Barchester novels, the Palliser novels, Trollope as travel writer, Trollope as magazine editor, as post office official, and so on. There is a lot to be said for adopting a simple, well-recognised approach and some of the most successful exhibitions mounted have explored the obvious in an admirable way. Even when this is done, though, it is possible (at any rate in the libraries rich in resources) to select exhibition items which will be fresh and unfamiliar: one of the delights of the Bibliothèque Nationale's exhibition *Le livre* in 1972 was in its showing of things which one had not seen in the King's Library or elsewhere.

Equally, however, there is much to be said for the exhibition which cuts across established themes and classifications and presents what may be thoroughly familiar books in unfamiliar juxtapositions. When successful, it will of course create its own familiar pattern: the 1963 *Printing and the mind of man* show, by grouping together a selection of those printed works 'which might be called the decisive battles against ignorance and darkness in the history of man' was setting a pattern for what has since become commonplace in attitudes to the history of printing. The danger with this sort of approach of course, is that it can become a striving after novely for novelty's sake, and not really contribute to a fresh understanding at all.

By extension to the investigation of the bibliographical resources of the library, the basic planning of the exhibition demands a thorough examination of the physical resources at one's command. If one cannot satisfactorily display more than a couple of dozen folios satisfactorily, planning will be constricted by this, however much the theme might call for twice the number. Even though the library possesses enough display equipment of the right kind, one has also to consider whether its layout is such that it permits a logical development of the theme: whether purposeful visitors to the show, having armed themselves with catalogues, can start their tour with item one and go through to the end in a coherent sequence with no backtracking—something surprisingly difficult to achieve.

Good display techniques will demand much more than has already been indicated, calling not only for the writing of the programme notes to accompany the books being displayed, but also for the provision of much ancillary material. This will include blown up photographs, for example, and a number of things best described as museum items. One will not perhaps normally have such things in a library, but the use of some non-bookish objects, to illustrate something about the books on show, can add powerfully to the impact of the exhibition upon the visitor. (4) At one end of the scale there will be things connected with the books shown, such as an engraver's burins and blocks shown with a book opened at the impression of one of the blocks, with blown-up reproductions of an engraver at work for added effect. Or for an exhibition on, say, books on coffee, to have some of the different kinds of coffee beans, plus blow-ups of illustrations of plantations, coffeehouse scenes and so forth could be appropriate.

How far one should go with such things when they are provided not to illustrate the books on show, or the subjects that the books deal with, but merely for window-dressing is a moot point. If in mounting an exhibition of books on anatomy, one could easily lay hands on a skull, then it could prove useful. But it would not be worth spending much time and trouble on hunting for one. The danger of being precious and affected becomes much greater when too much attention is devoted to the window-dressing side of the display.

In addition to the organisation of the exhibition itself, much extra work is needful for publicity. So much work has to go into a full-scale exhibition that it is not worthwhile unless the show can be mounted

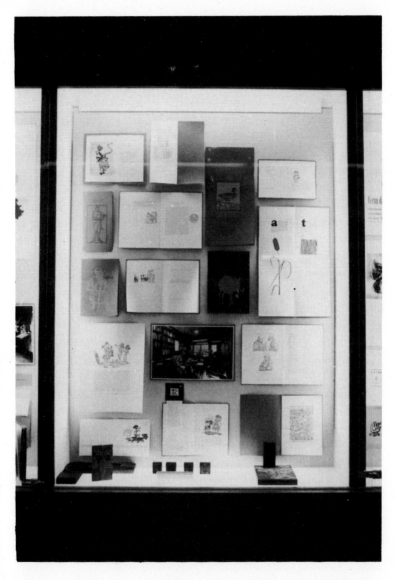

Plate 6: Private Press Exhibition, Wichita 1971. Wall display case; unlabelled and perhaps overcrowded, but well lighted and arranged and showing good use of artists' blocks to add interest to the display.

for a reasonable period of time, and unless it can be given enough publicity for those likely to be interested in attending to know that the show is on. Not infrequently libraries will take the opportunity of adding a lecture to the exhibition; or perhaps a series of lectures related to the theme of the show. The administrative problems in this (discussed below) are many and considerable, but such lectures can be very useful in attracting people to the exhibition who might otherwise not attend, in gaining press and radio or television publicity, and not least in obtaining material for the library's publication. This last aspect of the library's role is discussed in the next chapter.

Loan exhibitions
On some occasions it may well be desirable that the library mount an exhibition on a particular theme, but it will be unable to do so entirely from its own resources. Sometimes, indeed, it may mount a show which will be drawn entirely from other collections—of a private collector interested in the library's work, or of several libraries which can collectively mount a show of national or international importance. Such libraries as the Bibliothèque Nationale, Bodley or the British Museum frequently use material they have borrowed for exhibitions; it should not be thought that this is a practice limited to the small library.

Whenever a proposed exhibition is to include books obtained on loan, a much longer planning period is needed. Personal contacts will be necessary to enlist first the sympathy and then the practical support of the libraries (whether institutional or private) from whom one is asking a considerable favour, fraught with all sorts of dangers of damage or loss to the books they may lend. The owners must be satisfied that the personnel of the borrowing institution will handle the material with proper care, that adequate measures for its security will be taken while it is in transit as well as during the exhibition, and of course that the temporary departure of the books from their own collections will not cause difficulties to their own users.

In short, such arrangements can only well be arranged on personal acquaintance basis, where the lender will be satisfied because the rare books librarian requesting the loan is putting his own professional reputation at stake as guarantee. The librarian organising such an exhibition will have a good deal of travelling as well as correspondence in these planning stages. In many cases, having reached agreement in principle with one of the libraries prepared to lend material, he will then have to spend some time in selecting the books to be borrowed: this can be done only when the planning is at a sufficiently advanced stage for him to say with precision how many books of such and such sizes he will need. He will also have to prepare his catalogue notes in advance, so that the catalogues can be put to press before the loaned items are in his charge.

Many lending libraries will require a written agreement on the terms of loan, and it is wise for the borrowing library to make this an element from the first stage of negotiations. Typically, this agreement will contain a number of clauses:

(i) that the lending institution agrees to lend certain named and valued books for a stated period;

(ii) that the borrowing library undertakes collection and return of the books personally by named staff and by agreed modes of transport, and undertakes not to allow the books to be passed elsewhere without prior permission in writing from the lender;(5)

(iii) that the books lent will be exhibited only in display cases of mutually agreed design, and in agreed conditions of security;(6)

(iv) that the material borrowed will be insured for its full value from the time of departure to the time of its return to the lending institution.

Conditions of this sort can impose a considerable strain not only on the rare books librarian and his immediate staff, but also on bursars, registrars and others who will be concerned with the insurance, staffing, security, transport and related matters. The first time one attempts to organise such a show one encounters many difficulties: explaining to the official why the ordinary interlibrary loan methods will not suffice in this instance; why special insurance policies are necessary and so forth. All this takes time, but it is time well spent: there is no point in trying to cut corners, and no librarian if wise will agree to anything less than the sort of conditions listed above. One has heard enough horror stories, of rare books being returned from loan in a jiffy bag sent by unregistered post, (and others of the same kind), to appreciate the precautions that are needful when one is borrowing or lending.

Preparing the exhibition

Mounting the exhibition, arranging the books in the cases and writing the programme notes, will take a lot of time and thought. Whatever catalogues or other publications may be prepared for the exhibition, the librarian will need for his own current use and future reference a complete list of the exhibits and a plan showing precisely where each is exhibited, plus a copy of the descriptive note which accompanies each exhibit. In my experience this is very useful even when a catalogue is published, since one often receives enquiries about the exhibition which can be answered far more readily from the plan than from the catalogue. Further, it is by no means unusual (however undesirable) for one's plans for the exhibition to require last minute modification, after the catalogues have been prepared, and in that case the plan and accompanying notes will be the only accurate record of what was actually shown. And since it is often desirable to include slightly different information on the notes which accompany the exhibits, or information arranged differently from its catalogue presentation, such a record is additionally important.

If the exhibition is to be visited by a larger public than the normal habitués of shows put on in the library, it is vital that suitable announcements be sent long in advance to appropriate sources. Naturally these will vary according to the theme and location of the exhibition, but they will certainly include journals like *AB bookman's weekly, Bibliography newsletter. The book collector* and societies concerned with the subject. The need for this publicity is self-evident: if a society's newsletter appears quarterly there is little chance of getting the publicity before the show opens unless the editor receives your press release at least six months before the opening date. Publicity so far in advance may of course have to be limited to a fairly brief statement of the scope and intention of the show, though additional information (on lectures, for example) should always be given if available.

Further advance press releases will be prepared shortly before the exhibition's opening, and distributed to local and national newspapers, radio stations and so forth as appropriate. Local papers in particular will often run a feature on such exhibitions which are based very closely on the press releases, so it is worth taking a lot of trouble with them, and providing photographs of some of the key exhibits for their use.

A further form of publicity is of course the poster. Massive public display of posters for exhibitions is probably beyond the reach of most libraries of less than national standing, but the distribution of posters (which can be quite small in size) on a wide scale is valuable. Valuable because many libraries and museums have the useful custom of displaying one another's posters, and because the despatch of posters to appropriate institutions can have very positive results—I have known of several instances where the circulation of Bodley's exhibition posters to library schools has led to the organisation of student visits specifically to view that exhibition.

The production of posters is not particularly cheap, and certainly must not appear so. It can have the advantage of using the same central motif as will be used on the catalogue and in the exhibition itself, so that a recognisable style pervades the whole. At times it is possible to invoke the aid of (for instance) the local school of art, in such design work. Through such means some very effective posters in two-or three-colour silkscreen or other media can often be produced for a very modest outlay.

It is normal practice to have a private viewing, or an official opening of the exhibition, which can in itself be of further publicity value. Obviously all those who have aided the show, by the loan of materials or services, will be invited to this; as will others to whom the exhibition will be of special interest—the 'friends of the library', the library committee, members of local societies and so forth. To cast one's net widely in sending out invitations to such gatherings is no bad thing: I have known several instances in which (for example) university lecturers having come to a private view out of a sense of curiosity have subsequently returned with student parties to see the public exhibition.

129

Special lectures

The value of having a series of lectures related to the theme of the exhibition has already been mentioned. These may be for the purpose of

Plate 7:   A poster for the Klingspor Museum, Offenbach-a-M.

enriching the exhibition (and of course increasing its publicity value) by drawing on the services of those who are established national figures in that subject field; they may also be used to provide a platform for those whose reputation is more localised but who are contributing usefully to the area of study. If several lectures are planned for the course of the exhibition, it is in many instances appropriate to seek a mixture of the two types.

There are several problems to consider in this. Professor X may be the world authority on Assyrian woodwind instruments, on which he writes with clarity and wit. But can he *lecture*? To have a star lecture which is a failure can cast a blight over the whole exhibition, and certainly dissuade those who attended his talk from ever coming to other lectures put on by your library. Will the financial regulations of your institution permit you to offer a realistic fee? In many instances people in Britain are still prepared to come to talk for a fee which does little more than cover their hotel and travelling expenses—which is just as well, since in many institutions the regulations are such that this is all they can be paid. One feels pretty cheap at asking a man to give up perhaps two days of his time for a fee of twelve guineas or so, though fortunately enough scholars are still sufficiently missionaries in spirit (or happy enough to be given the chance of riding a hobbyhorse) to disregard the derisory financial rewards. In North America a more realistic attitude to fees applies, but this introduces fresh complications: is the prestige of Dr Y, whom you know to be a $500 fee man, sufficiently greater than that of Professor Z, who might come to you for a couple of hundred dollars less?

Briefing the special lecturer on the scope, level and timing of his lecture, and on relating it to the exhibition which he may not yet have seen, can also present difficulties. Naturally one will be required to meet him from plane or train, attend to his hotel accommodation, lunch him and so forth, as well as look after the mechanics of his lecture and see that he receives his fee and expenses promptly. All simple matters of hospitality, but often difficult to organise when the rare books librarian may have other urgent matters concerning the exhibition (to say nothing of his routine work) which should be receiving his attention.

The brief notes above have not mentioned some of the basic administrative problems, such as the availability of a suitable lecture room with all necessary audio-visual equipment, of tickets to lectures and so forth. But they should have indicated how the organisation of a lecture series can add a fresh dimension to the exhaustion that the rare books librarian is likely to feel after arranging a loan exhibition. But it is well worth it for the professional satisfaction one receives from a lecture which is a success with the audience, for the publicity for the collection and its work which is generated by such occasions, and for the personal contacts which one forms with the guest lecturers.

Fellowships
An aspect of organising the library's collections for use which should not be neglected is that which is concerned with encouraging the use of the materials by outside scholars. In many cases when the rare book

collection is part of a larger institution, it may be felt that the opportunities for scholars who wish to use the collections are already sufficient. In many instances, however, particularly when the library is an independent one, or is remote from main centres of learning, it is very desirable that the library should have some funds at its command to assist with the living and transport costs of those who are likely to make good use of the research materials in the collection. In other words, the library pays the scholar to work in it.

Naturally the money available for such assistance is always limited, but some libraries will have a series of research fellowships to assist those who might otherwise be unable to afford to work there. Some of these fellowships (like those at Gregynog, or at the American Antiquarian Society) will permit a scholar to take up residence for a limited period; sometimes the assistance will be slighter, but permit the recipient to cover part of his hotel bills for a week, or something of that nature. The amount involved will never be large, but it may well make the difference between scholarly exploitation of the material (which will redound to the credit of the library as well as the scholar) and its continuing unused. When libraries are able to obtain funds for such fellowships, a policy for administering them will be devised similar to that for obtaining scholarships in universities: the fellowship will be advertised, and on the basis of the applications (which will describe in detail the type and purpose of the research work to be undertaken, and the end-product envisaged) a selection committee will decide which of the applications should receive support.

Recipients of such fellowships will often have some conditions attached to their awards. That they should be in residence for the duration of the award is a common one, and may imply no more than that some of their special knowledge and research techniques may rub off on the library staff and students with whom they will come into informal contact. Sometimes there are more formal requirements, such as advice on stockbuilding, or a lecture or tutorial sessions with students. A frequent condition, tacitly understood, is that the press or learned journal with which the library is connected may have first refusal of any publication which results from the research undertaken.

References

1 A number of stands and blocks, preferably of transparent plastic, will be needed for this. The leaves of books may be held flat with bands of cellulose acetate.

2 The arrangement of these with the cases, as in the British Museum's Stanley Morison exhibition in 1971, enables the library to arrange a small intimate exhibition without interfering with larger continuing exhibitions in the same hall.

3 Libraries sometimes have rules which prevent readers' consultation of books which are on exhibition. This may at times be justified for books which are in special exhibitions, at any rate for regular readers; but if a reader has come specifically to consult that volume, and his research will be stultified by its lack, it is clearly wrong to deny him its use just because it is a nuisance for the library staff and will make a hole in the exhibition.

4 An extreme instance (but a very effective one) is to be seen in the display area of the Institute of Jamaica, where the jaws of a shark are displayed together with some ships' papers which were retrieved from them in 1799. (The story of 'The shark papers' is well told by Clinton Black in his *Tales of old Jamaica* London, Collins, 1966).

5 Several rare book librarians have spoken bitterly to me about books which they have lent, and which—the exhibition proving a success, and requests for it to be shown elsewhere having been considerable—the borrowing institution has calmly sent on as a part of the show.

6 In one instance which I recall vividly, in order to comply with the lender's requirements it was necessary to move a camp bed into the library and for the personnel to take it in shifts to sleep there, so that there was twenty-four hour surveillance. Fortunately the exhibition was not on for very long.

133

Chapter X
Publicity and publications

Provided they are imaginatively planned and competently organised—and provided one is lucky—the special exhibitions and lecture programmes described in the last chapter will be successful. Successful in the sense of earning some publicity for the rare book collections, and also in providing a satisfying educational and cultural experience for those who attended the lectures or viewed the exhibition.

This is not enough in any of these cases. The favourable publicity which accrues to a research collection is very slow to develop if it depends solely on word of mouth or press reports. The University of Barset may, one has read in the news and commentary columns of the *Book collector* or the *Times Literary supplement*, mount some outstandingly good exhibitions, and have had lecture series which are highly regarded. But this won't mean much to the scholar working in relevant fields if he has not been to Barchester to see the exhibitions and listen to the talks, unless some method is adopted of reaching a wider audience. Even for those who have been fortunate enough to attend, after a period of time both exhibition and talks will have faded into a vague remembrance of things past unless the library provides means of keeping recollection lively.

Publications built around exhibitions will then have a threefold purpose: i) to serve as a guide to those visiting the exhibition, to explain its purpose and arrangement and to bring out the significance of the various items on display—telling the visitor what to look at, and why; ii) to act as an aide-memoire for those who have seen the exhibition; iii) to be a substitute for a visit to the exhibition for those unable to view it; and by extension to serve as a permanent reference book which will preserve the imagination and learning which went into the preparation of the show. The different purposes may be met by a number of different publications perhaps, better than by one which tries to serve all purposes. Many visitors to exhibitions, after all, are not concerned particularly with the subject of the exhibition, and will not wish to pay a rather high price for a detailed illustrated catalogue. For their purpose a simple handlist of the exhibits, with a brief introductory note, will be quite adequate. It will sufficiently clarify the arrangement of the exhibition and enable the visitor to find his way around the display cases in logical order. Such handlists can be prepared simply enough, and if reproduced by duplicating or office offset are cheap enough for the library to be able to provide copies at a nominal charge or better still free—a not unimportant point to consider when one perhaps expects the exhibition to be visited by school parties.

Even though the institution's finances may demand that a charge of a few pence is made for such handlists, there will be some visitors unable or unwilling to pay the cost. There is no excuse, when arranging and labelling the exhibits, for putting the visitor who does not have the guide at a disadvantage by failing to include as much information on the labels as is included in the guide or catalogue. Equally there is no reason good enough for failing to provide a handlist of the exhibits, although too frequently this happens. There may be plenty of reasons—particularly for the small relatively informal exhibition—that it is inconvenient to prepare a list; certainly at times there will be adequate excuses for a list being delayed in production, or being temporarily out of stock, but to my mind an exhibition mounted without some handlist for the visitor is a demonstration of professional inadequacy.

The work which is intended for reference will be different in kind. As one hopes that it will have permanent value a more durable form of physical production is desirable in place of the duplicated stapled sheets which may serve for a handlist. Illustrations are desirable, particularly for the unique items and representative works in the show for which illustrations are not easily found elsewhere. The method of reproduction used for these illustrations will of course be dictated by the funds available and the price which is to be set on the publication. When funds are minuscule one can make effective use of gestefax stencils or offset litho reproductions from xerox; if on the other hand one can afford four-colour gravure, as the Hunt Library did for some of the tipped-in plates in its magnificent *Catalogue of Redoutéana* (Pittsburgh, 1963) so much the better.

The catalogue must include not only the list of exhibits with annotations, but some prefatory matter which will put the annotated entries into context. This may take the form of a general essay on the subject of the exhibition, which is especially appropriate and useful if the published references to the subject are inaccessible, or if the exhibition's arrangement presents the subject in an unfamiliar way. Such essays may on appropriate occasions be commissioned from outside authorities: the splendid catalogue of the equally splendid Pierpont Morgan Library exhibition, *The art of the printed book 1455–1955* (New York, 1973) for example, is prefaced by a fifty one page essay on 'The great printers and their books' by Joseph Blumenthal. The *Catalogue of Redoutéana*, already referred to, includes a thirty-two page account of Redouté's life by Dr Frans Stafleu of Utrecht, as well as shorter introductions written by members of the Hunt staff to the sections listing books illustrated by Redouté, and his drawings, paintings and prints. This catalogue concludes with a section on letters by Redouté, which was prepared originally for a publication celebrating the centenary of the Societé Royale de Belgique. Quite regardless of the magnificent physical production of the catalogue, the formidable concentration of scholarship it contains makes it an outstanding reference book.

The same is true of the volume *Siberch celebrations 1521–1971* produced by the University Printing House in Cambridge in 1971. It *is* a catalogue of the exhibition 'From Caxton to Siberch' which was held in the University Library, but this is only one third of the whole; the rest of the volume containing essays by various hands on books in sixteenth century Cambridge, printing in Siberch's time, on contemporary literacy and on Siberch himself, plus the text of William Rastell's 'Interlude of the four elements' which was performed as part of the celebrations at Cambridge. In other words, the need for an exhibition catalogue was used as a peg on which to hang many other matters of relevance and interest, resulting in an unusual but very effective miscellany.

At times the need to provide an introduction to the subject can

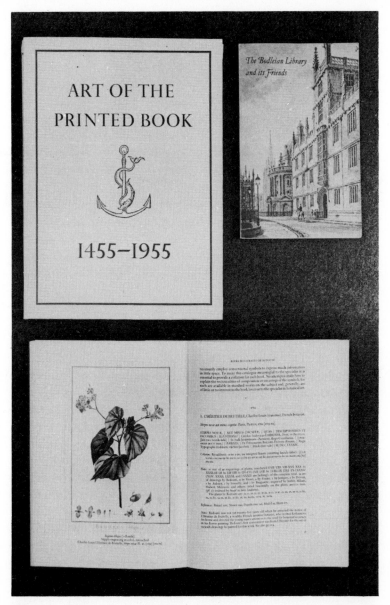

Plate 8: Three well designed exhibition catalogues: Pierpont Morgan Library, Bodleian Library and the Hunt Botanical Library's *Redoutéana*.

persuade a library to produce a pamphlet separate from the catalogue proper. The Library of Congress described its book *Papermaking, art and craft* (Washington, 1968) as 'an account derived from the exhibition' and it is certainly *not* a catalogue at all, but an outstanding short introduction to the subject. On a much slighter level the same sort of approach was adopted by the British Museum with its leaflet *Wilkes and liberty* (London, 1969) produced for the Museum's exhibition celebrating the bicentenary of Wilkes' expulsion from the House of Commons. Another was undertaken by Loughborough Library School, with its *The private press: handbook to an exhibition* (Loughborough, 1968). The arguments behind its production were that at the time there was no good cheap general introduction to the subject available for students; that relatively few general readers believe that a prefatory essay in a catalogue is intended for separate reading; and that the peculiarities of library classification reasonably tend to conceal such essays by classing the catalogues with bibliographies rather than the subjects of the exhibition. Though it was well enough received to have justified the experiment, the Loughborough handbook did not meet the need for a proper catalogue of the exhibition, and it is noticeable that they reverted to a conventional catalogue for their next show, *Natural history illustration* (1969).

Usually, from a commendable sense of modesty in the rare books staff, catalogues are put out as under the collective authorship of the institution. This is very proper, since the work of organising an exhibition tends to be spread among various members of staff. However, such anonymity can be taken too far.(1) Usually the catalogue's preface or acknowledgements will indicate those members of staff (or outside advisers) most concerned in the organisation of the show, and the writing of the catalogue, which will enable the interested scholar to make contact directly with the right person.(2) But even this partial degree of anonymity can have disadvantages, since it makes it much less likely that the scholar undertaking a literature search via the names of authors on his subject will find entries under their names for catalogues they have prepared. If I am interested in the book illustrator John Minton, for example, I might well know that Mr Rigby Graham is an authority on Minton's work, but would I find an entry under his name for the catalogue of the Minton exhibition which he organised at Leicester College of Art in 1967? I doubt it.

For this reason, and for the equally good one of giving credit where credit is due, the catalogue which has on its titlepage as authors the names of those responsible for organising the exhibition and writing the catalogue, is to be preferred. Such are the Huntington Library's *Great books in great editions* by Roland Baughman and Robert O Schad San Marino, Calif, 1954; 2nd ed 1965, or the Pierpont Morgan Library's *Bookbindings by T J Cobden-Sanderson* by Frederick B Adams New York, 1969 or Mr Howard Nixon's swansong at the British Museum *English restoration bookbindings: Samuel Mearne and his contemporaries* London, 1974.

The level to which the catalogue aspires will be dictated partly by the scale of the exhibition: if for example one were to mount a show on the art of the book one would need the resources of the Bibliothèque Nationale or the Morgan Library to hope to produce a catalogue which would take a position as one of the standard reference books on the subject (as is the case with both these catalogues). On the other hand, a relatively small-sized exhibition and catalogue dealing with a restricted subject area can produce work of the highest level. Despite the existence of full-scale biographies of Stanley Morison, for instance, the catalogues of the exhibition *Stanley Morison et la tradition typographique* (Brussels/The Hague, 1966) or the British Museum's *Stanley Morison, a portrait* (London, 1971) are of enduring value—not only because they are exceptionally well annotated and illustrated catalogues, but because the different arrangement adopted for these exhibitions reveal facets of the subject in ways not brought out so vividly in the other works.

Some of the catalogues produced by the Hunt Botanical Library although very modest in size serve as the best guides to their subjects. The *Redoutéana* catalogue is in the same class as the Morison catalogues; its catalogues *Botanical illustrations by Anne Ophelia Todd Dowden* Pittsburgh, 1965 or George Lawrence's *20th century botanical art and illustration* Pittsburgh, 1969 are excellent instances of the small-scale exhibition catalogue of enduring value.(3) One can easily suggest other instances in which catalogues of exhibitions very modest in extent would be permanent contributions of merit. (4)

Some exhibitions of importance are designed deliberately for showing at several different centres. This is a mode which presents some difficulties in organisation, but has the obvious advantage of enabling more people to visit the show—as for example the annual Western Books show mounted in both Los Angeles and San Francisco. One of the most successful of such shows was the touring exhibition of some of Bodley's treasures in the United States in 1969–70; the catalogue, *The Bodleian Library and its friends*, was particularly attractive and itself an interesting example of international cooperation, having been printed in Connecticut from filmset material produced in Oxford.

As far as the production of the catalogues is concerned, touring shows normally present difficulties only when the exhibition is to cross linguistic boundaries, when one has to choose between producing different editions or a bilingual or even polyglot text. The solution adopted in the Low Countries, where the Royal Libraries in Brussels and the Hague, and the Plantin-Moretus Museum in Antwerp often cooperate in this way, is to go for separate editions. This was the case with the Morison exhibition already referred to, and for those on the *Officina Bodoni* (1965) and *Herman Zapf* (1962)—these two catalogues not only being in French and Dutch editions, but printed in Italy and Germany respectively. This cooperation between Belgium and Holland is obviously useful for the libraries concerned, and also for the sale of catalogues, as the potential international market for catalogues in French is obviously greater than for the Dutch texts.

On some occasions the library may act as host for meetings of bibliographic or book-collecting societies. The exhibition catalogues produced for such occasions tend (as one would expect) to be unusual in one way or another, being prepared by the expert for the expert. They range from the British Museum's large folio *English book illustration 966–1846* (produced for the Fourth International Congress of Bibliophiles, 1965) to the Newberry Library's double-ended dual *Catalogue of . . . Western materials from the Graff collection/Books and manuscripts from the Silver collection* (for the Grolier Club visit, 1965). My own favourite is that produced by the Houghton Library at Harvard for the Bibliographical Society of America's meeting there in 1962:

Bibliotheca chimaerica: a catalogue of an exhibition of catalogues of imaginary books. Prepared 'with the aid of those members of the Houghton Library staff who appreciate the accumulation of not very useful information' it is a splendid example of scholarly humour.

Periodicals

Many of the larger research libraries will have their own regular journal. *The Bodleian Library record, Harvard Library bulletin, Bulletin of the New York Public Library, The Long Room, Huntia* are examples of the genre. The work of such journals is not limited to the particular library's rare book departments, though these will often preponderate.

To have a regular journal of this kind offers some significant advantages: i) in enabling the library to publicise new acquisitions, new services etc.; ii) in providing a convenient and appropriate vehicle for the publication of research articles based on the study of materials in the library's collections, whether written by visiting scholars or by members of the library staff; iii) in providing a convenient means of issuing the texts of some of the special lectures given at the library; iv) as a channel of communication with regular users of the library, with librarians of other are book collections, and those interested in the work of the library—the 'Friends of the Library'—to whom the journal can be supplied as some return for their subscriptions; v) in providing the library with a regular publication which is useful for exchange purposes.

The contents of these journals often affords a useful source of publicity for the library, since they are frequently reviewed or noticed by eg *Times literary supplement, Book collector, The library*. But despite their advantages, one cannot lightly embark on their publication. There is the purely financial consideration that they will almost certainly cost substantially more to produce than they will bring in from subscriptions (a hard fact which has caused more than one such journal of recognised merit to be discontinued), and also the fact that the labour of editing such a regular journal adds very considerably to the workload of the staff of the rare book department. A compromise in terms of both workload and finance is to have an irregular bulletin or newsletter which may be produced very simply (duplicated if need be) and only when the occasion demands. Such a publication, like the *Library notes* produced by the Library of the Royal Commonwealth Society, can meet many of the needs of the library, though it is obviously not as suitable a medium for publishing the texts of lectures or other material emanating from outside.

Library catalogues
Valuable though many exhibition catalogues and library bulletins are, they can seldom have the long-term continuing usefulness as reference tools which the published catalogues of substantial collections of rare books will possess. Sometimes a library's catalogues of its collections lends itself well to piecemeal publication, like the Manchester catalogue of private press books described in Chapter IV. For some of the largest research libraries, this publication in parts will be the most useful mode; indeed the only practicable one if the special types of cataloguing which is demanded by the nature of the material is to be provided. The two volumes on *French sixteenth century books* in the collection of the Department of Graphic Arts at Harvard (Cambridge, Mass, 1964) is an instance of such a special catalogue, supremely well done.

There may well be other instances in which distinct and complete units exist in the collection, even more clearly defined than this Harvard example, and for these a separately published catalogue is almost essential. *Robert Addison's library, a short-title catalogue of the books brought to Upper Canada in 1792* Hamilton, McMaster University for the Synod of Niagara, 1967 or Shropshire County Library's *Catalogue of books from parochial libraries in Shropshire* London, 1971 typify this group.

In some cases, because of a library's wealth of material in a subject, the comprehensive catalogue of the collection will form one of the best bibliographies of that subject that could exist. The cost of typesetting and conventional proofreading and printing for a catalogue of this kind will be enormous, even for one far more modest in typographic terms than the Harvard or Hunt Catalogues. However, modern methods of reproducing existing catalogue entries acceptably in volume form—as seen in the British Museum's *General catalogue* and

NUC pre-1956 imprints—have enabled such firms as Mansell or G K Hall to develop a specialisation in this type of bibliographical publishing at reasonable cost. Their work is not a typographical delight, but it is perfectly useable and in some instances preferable to the catalogues from which their volumes have been derived. When seeking to publish large scale catalogues, the research library is likely to work through such agencies. To have one's catalogues published through ordinary publishing/booktrade channels obviously offers considerable advantages.

Other publications

It is the practice of some libraries to publish the texts of public lectures as an irregular series of separate pamphlets. This has the advantage, of course, of making access to the lectures rather easier than when they are published in a journal. The University of California has done particularly good work in this way, with the texts of the Howel/ Zeitlin & Ver Brugge annual lectures, such as Lawrence Clark Powell's *Bibliographers of the Golden State* (1967), A N L Munby's *The history and bibliography of science in England 1833–1845* (1968), Frederick B Adams's *The uses of provenance* (1969) or Divid Foxon's *Thoughts on the history and future of bibliographical description* (1970). UCLA's rare book library, the William Andrews Clark Memorial Library, has also published some very important work from papers presented at some of its seminars, such as Carey S Bliss on *Joseph Moxon* (1965), Fredson Bowers and Lyle H Wright on *Bibliography* (1966), or James D Hart and Ward Ritchie on *Influences on California printing* (1970). The importance of these publications as contributions to the literature of their subjects is very considerable.

As well as the regular exhibition catalogues, journals, and seminar papers described above, there are several other categories of publication which are appropriate for a rare book library to issue. There are brief guides to the history of the library, like that put out by the Folger Shakespeare Library (Washington, 1968) or the short account of *Henry Edwards Huntington* put out by the Huntington Library (San Marino, 1968). At the other end of the scale for publications about the library is the princely *The Houghton Library 1942–1967; a selection of books*

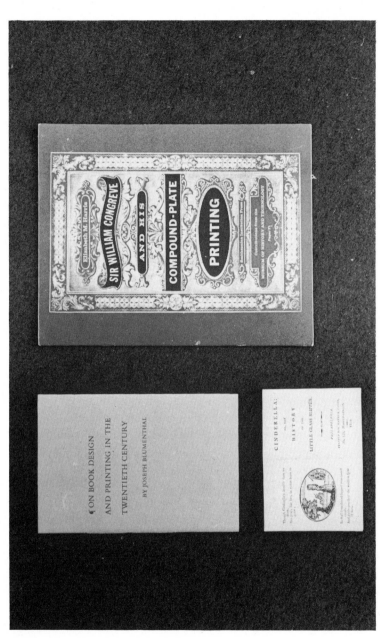

Plate 9: Rare book library publications: The text of a public lecture (UCLA), a short monograph from the Smithsonian, and the Huntington Library's reprint of the first American edition of *Cinderella*.

and manuscripts in Harvard collections Cambridge, Mass, 1967 or the almost equally splendid *Bibliothèque Royale, memorial 1559–1969* produced to celebrate the library's move into its new buildings in Brussels in 1969. There are the pamphlets put out to describe some of a library's treasures, like Tönnes Kleberg's *Codex Argenteus: the Silver Bible at Uppsala* Uppsala, 1962. Often there will be a series of such, like the Bodleian Library picture books.

Beyond this is a whole range of publications which may be aimed at the serious student, but may equally be intended for the casual visitor. One type quite often encountered is the facsimile edition: Cambridge University Library's edition of Hornschuch's *Orthotypographia 1608* (1972) as the first of the Library's Historical Bibliography series, is clearly for the scholarly market. The Huntington's facsimile of the only known copy of the first American edition of *Cinderella*, measuring 4″ × 2¾″, and prettily got up in marbled paper covers, is just as clearly for impulse buying by the casual visitor. Other publications will include postcards and lettercards and greetings cards showing pages or plates from some of the important books in the collection; or posters and full-size colour facsimiles of prints and maps. La Casa del Libro in Puerto Rico, for instance, which is housed in one of the charming old Spanish houses in San Juan, offers greetings cards bearing an elegant silkscreen reproduction of the street facade of the house, and also has a number of exciting calligraphic posters. The New York Public Library, among its many other publications offers a poster illustrating its outstanding collection of 19th century display types; from the Plantin-Moretus Museum one can buy a broadside of a poem written by Plantin, set in his types and printed on one of the old handpresses on display.

Publications need not, of course, be limited to these traditional forms. From time to time Birmingham Reference Library has sold casts of its slate-engraving by John Baskerville, for instance. One of the really excellent features of the memorable exhibition *Fine bindings 1500–1700 from Oxford libraries*, which the Bodleian Library mounted in the Divinity Schools at Oxford in 1968, was that it was possible to buy for a modest price slides of every exhibit shown. To provide slides of at least a selection of the important books and prints shown

LE BONHEUR
DE CE MONDE.

SONNET.

AVoir une maison commode, propre & belle,
Un jardin tapissé d'espaliers odorans,
Des fruits, d'excellent vin, peu de train, peu d'enfans,
Posseder seul, sans bruit, une femme fidele.

N'avoir dettes, amour, ni procés, ni querelle,
Ni de partage à faire avecque ses parens,
Se contenter de peu, n'esperer rien des Grands,
Regler tous ses desseins sur un juste modele.

Vivre avecque franchise & sans ambition,
S'adonner sans scrupule à la devotion,
Domter ses passions, les rendre obeïssantes.

Conserver l'esprit libre, & le jugement fort,
Dire son Chapelet en cultivant ses entes,
C'est attendre chez soi bien doucement la mort.

Sonnet composé par Christophe PLANTIN, imprimé avec le matériel de la célèbre Archi-typographie.

This letter R demonstrates the main
principles behind the shaping of the design
called Dartmouth: emphatically waisted strokes, with
strong, square-ended serifs and clearly-defined counters;
perfect for incising on stone or wood. Originally conceived for some carved teak panels in the Hopkins
Center at Dartmouth College, New Hampshire,
it was later adapted as a type-face.

Prepared by Will Carter as a Keepsake on the occasion of his lecture at UCLA in the series Taste in Typography, 29th April 1969

Plate 10:   Rare book library keepsakes: left, UCLA; right Plantin-Moretus Museum, Antwerp.

in exhibitions, and to have them available for some of the other important items the library possesses, is very desirable in any publications policy.

Funding of publications
Though the actual production costs may be hidden, even the most modest publication which the library is going to produce is going to cost something, while at the other end of the scale straight production costs for paper, blockmaking, printing and binding may well run into thousands of pounds.

Whatever the scale of the operations, some planning is vital if the library's publication programme is to have a chance of success. The small library, with a very modest programme, may well have more administrative problems, and difficulty in persuading financial authorities to agree to certain operating procedures, than will be the case in a larger institution for which publishing will be a standard function.

What one has to aim for is the creation of a special publications fund with a revolving budget: that is, the creation of a special allocation in the library's funds, which can be carried forward from year to year, and to which will be credited the proceeds of the sales of all catalogues and other publications.(5) If one is fortunate, and has planned well, some publications will strike a receptive market and pay for themselves in a relatively short while; others will sell so slowly that they will never be successes in commercial terms. Persuading finance officers that despite this they should be produced because of the intangible benefits they bring the library in publicity and prestige (as well, one hopes, as being of service to scholarship) can be an uphill task. Unless one can subsidise the commercial failures from the profitable publications, the publishing programme will be seen simply as a drain on resources, and as one of the first things to be jettisoned in times of financial stringency.

The heaviest cost in catalogue publishing is usually that of blockmaking: a few pages of half-tones though they may add to a publication's attractiveness will add even more to the cost, and one has to weigh the greater reader-appeal against the disincentive to buy which

147

the necessarily higher price will create. Sometimes it is possible to borrow blocks from other sources; alternatively the use of line-blocks is relatively cheap and for some types of work can be just as satisfactory as the half-tone.

If one can find locally a small printing firm interested in the library's work, and which has facilities for good quality printing, it is ideal, but frequently it will be necessary to go further afield. At times this can have positive advantages: for Loughborough's *The private press* (1968), for instance, it was appropriate to have the handbook to the exhibition itself printed at a private press. Several of the blocks used to illustrate it were loaned for the purpose, which reduced the printing costs, and a number of other appropriate stratagems were resorted to as well. First, in addition to the ordinary copies in paper wrappers 150 signed and numbered copies were bound in cloth boards and offered for sale at a substantially higher price. Most orders received from libraries were (as anticipated) for the hardbound edition which quickly sold out, so that a large proportion of the total production cost was soon recouped. Secondly, the paperbound copies of the handbook were put on sale for the duration of the exhibition at a specially low price for personal buyers; a price only a little higher than the unit production cost, in fact. This proved a powerful inducement to students and other visitors who could (as it were) see their investment double in value within a week or so. To charge a lower price at exhibitions than for subsequent orders can be justified in several ways: the commercial expectation that this will stimulate sales (certainly the case in the Loughborough experiment) and therefore the cash inflow, and also the fact that invoicing and other book-keeping costs are kept at a minimum, while there is no outlay on postage and packing.

Naturally in calculating the size of the edition and in setting a price on the publication the fact that some free copies *must* be distributed will be kept in mind. Copies used for exchange purposes will of course be charged at the production cost. Free copies will as a matter of courtesy be distributed to those who have helped with the show by lending books or in other ways; the distinguished guests at the opening, and the press, must also be given copies. To allow one hundred copies, say, for this sort of free distribution is a fair rule of thumb, and one which will often leave some copies which the rare books librarian can present to important visitors and others. The cash investment in this sort of gesture is very slight; the goodwill which can be generated is worth far more to the library.

'*Friends of the library*'

One of the best ways of encouraging and fostering public interest in the rare book library and its services is through the organisation of a group of friends of the library. Such groups are commoner in North America than in Britain, possibly because the British are less clubbable; but there are enough successful groups of this kind in Britain to suggest that the reason is to be found in the greater enthusiasm for such groups among librarians in the new world.

The groups may be brought into existence for two reasons. One is purely self-interest: as a convenient means of raising funds for the collection. The other is more concerned with the library's cultural and educational function, which can be served well by the creation of a group of those particularly interested in the subjects in which the library has special strength. There are plenty of men of modest means who may be concerned with bibliographic or bibliophile aspects of their subjects—and whether their interest is professional or amateur is no matter—who are unlikely ever to be able to offer much more than their interest and moral support, but who will benefit from their membership of such a group. Because of their personal commitment to the subject the group will tend to take on the character of an invisible college, and for this reason alone will be valuable to the library. There are also those who may be able to provide both money and services; men not specially interested in books or libraries but who—if they can be persuaded that the rare book library is a worthwhile cultural enterprise with which they should be connected—may prove to be very good friends of the library indeed. The ideal group is one in which wealthy businessmen and research students existing on a small grant can comfortably rub shoulders in a spirit of harmony, sustained by their common interest in the library and its collections.

The methods (and problems) of organising such groups have been described well by John Parker, whose account(7) should be read by

149

all contemplating the formation of one. Probably the best way of organising a body of such diverse membership is to have different categories of members, with a very low annual subscription for the ordinary members; payment of larger sums qualifying them for contributing or sustaining membership. The return which members will receive for their subscriptions will include such things as copies of exhibition catalogues, the library's journal, invitations to previews of the exhibitions and to public lectures, plus the intangible satisfaction of knowing they are supporting a worthwhile undertaking. It is well worth adding to these benefits, which after all they can obtain by other means than membership of the friends group, by providing some services which are available only to the members of the group. The production of a keepsake solely for the friends, to have an annual dinner and lecture which is for the friends and their guests only—these will not be very expensive or difficult to organise, but can add considerably to the attractions of taking out membership. For the non-bookman the impression that it is a rather special society, belonging to which confers some sort of cachet, can be a useful inducement. The publicity surrounding such events as the private views of the exhibitions or the dinner can be very helpful. A good many people are gratified by having their names listed as among those attending such functions, or by being able to say that they were talking to Sir Such and Such at the dinner—fairly innocent forms of vanity, from which the library can reap advantage.

References

1 It is not possible, for instance, to find out from the catalogue of the exhibition *La reliure romantique* shown at the Bibliothèque Royale, Brussels, in 1961, who arranged the show or wrote the catalogue entries. It seems a very accomplished piece of work, but obviously one could judge better with this information, and in addition would know to whom to write for further information on the subject.

2 Thus it is simple to find out precisely which of Bodley's staff was responsible for the exhibition of *The John Johnson collection* (Oxford 1971) or rather less easily which of the Bibliothèque Nationale's con-

servators were responsible for entries in *Le livre* catalogue (Paris 1972).

3 The value of the first is clear from its title; the latter serves as an excellent bio-bibliography of workers in this field.

4 If the Hamilton Public Library were to present a show on 'Printing in Bermuda' its catalogue would cover a subject on which very little has hitherto appeared. As another instance, since Loughborough Library School has the working papers of the Vine Press it could produce a monograph in its catalogue which would be of enduring use in private press studies.

5 Including, desirably, all royalty payments or other fees received from reprinting firms and others.

6 In Howard Nixon's *English restoration bindings* London, 1974 for instance, few private purchasers will pay £10 for the 125 monochrome plates included in the hardbound edition, as against the 75 pence charged for the paperback catalogue with one coloured plate. Yet a unit cost of 7p per plate is probably not unreasonable.

7 John Parker, 'The rare book library and the public' in *Rare book collections* ACRL monograph no 27, edited by H Richard Archer (Chicago, 1965) pp 108–20. Two other essays will also repay consideration: Robert O Schad, 'Friends of the Huntington Library' *Library trends* vol 5 no 4, April 1957, pp 483–8; and Frances J Brewer 'Friends of the Library and other benefactors' *Library trends* vol 9 no 1, April 1961, pp 453–65.

Chapter XI
The training of
rare book librarians

The foregoing chapters will have shown that the work to be undertaken by the librarian charged with the care and development of special collections is in many respects different from other types of library work. It calls for different skills, and to some extent a different professional ethos, from those requisite in many branches of librarianship.

In Britain, at any rate until very recently, there has been little attempt to provide any special training or educational facilities for the rare book librarian as such. The unfortunate split which developed between the academic and research libraries on the one hand, and public libraries on the other, with the very slow realisation by the former group that professional education as well as a good first degree, was desirable is now a matter of history. But it has had a number of unfortunate developments so far as the organisation of formal tuition in rare book librarianship is concerned, since for so many years the organisation of education for librarianship was typically (and entirely reasonably) geared towards the needs of the public librarian, in whose work special collections occupy but a small part of the whole.

The development of textbooks like John L Hobbs's *Libraries and the materials of local history* (1948) subsequently rewritten as his excellent *Local history and the library* London, Deutsch, 1962 shows that in some important respects training work was well done by the public librarian, and on the whole the local history collections in public libraries have been developed well.

This has been done, though, as a branch of public librarianship, *not* as an aspect of rare book librarianship. In so far as the Library Association's syllabus and examinations paid any attention at all to rare books and the special professional problems which they present, they have tended to do so in a rather theoretical and superficial way. Perfectly understandable, since the nongraduate studying for the ALA was never likely to have the task of cataloguing a large collection of early printed books, and those teaching him would seldom be doing so on the basis of extensive experience with such material.

For those who had first degrees and were working in research libraries, such education as there was in the care of rare books came through practical apprenticeship augmented by the excellent summer courses mounted from time to time through SCONUL. Valuable though these were, their impact was limited in the main to those from the larger research libraries: the possibilities for other than practical on-the-job training for those working in smaller collections has been very slight.

The recent pattern, in education for librarianship almost as much as in library work itself, has been towards the development of a subject approach, in place of the old functional division with its pyramidal concept. This is an approach to professional problems which in some respects brings the pattern of education closer to that which is desirable for rare book collections, since in their nature they tend to be subject departments. Equally frequently, however (at least in the larger library) rare book collections will include a good deal of miscellaneous material transferred to the department from the open shelves simply because of its rarity or market value. In short, some rare book collections are functional departments in the same sort of way that a serials section is a functional department, and a theoretical approach through the subject organisation of the library can cut straight across the practicalities of the work.

The basic education for a librarian intending to work with rare books should certainly be within the main disciplines covered by a library's collections. This is by no means an immutable rule; just as in the field of information science most of us can think of extremely competent practitioners who lack this basic requirement, so one can find many good rare books curators in charge of collections very remote from their own original areas of study. One will *normally* expect the intending librarian to have a good first degree(1) in an appropriate subject or combination of subjects. Determining what subjects are appropriate is not always a simple matter. Obviously for a botanical library a degree in botany will be an advantage. But so will a developed historical sense, and equally and often more important is the study of languages. The exploitation of a substantial botanical collection will demand a knowledge of English, Latin, French and German for a start; Spanish, Swedish, Dutch, Italian, Arabic, Greek immediately suggest themselves as only less important.

And the knowledge needed of these languages is not, of course, limited to an understanding of the modern or the classical tongues: wrestling with a sixteenth century herbal presents problems which one's study of Caesar or Cicero will not do much to solve. So just as the palaeographer must study mediaeval Latin and Norman French, so the rare book librarian will at times find that he needs sufficient knowledge to get by with, say, Middle High German.

This is clearly demanding the impossible, and though the librarian appointing an assistant for the rare book collection will hope for applications from polyglot prodigies, he will as a rule have to rest content with a demonstration that the candidate has some linguistic ability and clearly understands the need to improve it in various directions. In a penetrating but profoundly pessimistic account of the training of rare book librarians in the United States,(2) Rollo Silver commented that 'the college student today does not possess the training in languages, in the history of literature, in the disciplines of accuracy and clear communication which prevailed some years ago.' His analysis is not true only of the United States; changes in secondary schooling and university curricula everywhere, valuable though they may be for other reasons, militate strongly against the library school being able to build firmly upon a foundation of the virtues he lists. And in the custodian of a rare book collection a continuation of older qualities in scholarship, the painstaking accuracy of the antiquary, is particularly important.

So far as professional education is concerned, very few library schools offer courses on rare books or rare book librarianship as a part of the normal options available in programmes leading to the MLS, postgraduate diploma or similar qualifications. Once more it is partly an accident of history, in that in the move towards fulltime education for librarianship the schools have also moved towards the use of fulltime teaching staff whenever possible. Excellent though this has been,

154

it is a policy which militates against some of the specialisations which will attract only small numbers of students (like rare book librarianship) in that the specialists in these fields are unlikely to wish to move into a system in which most of their time will be demanded for work outside their chosen area.

For the student intending to specialise in this branch of librarianship, there are of course cognate courses which may be studied to advantage. Courses on local history librarianship; on the history of the book and of libraries; on the techniques of analytical and descriptive bibliography, will be particularly relevant. In some instances practical work with a bibliographical press will be useful. If courses on palaeography and archive work are offered, they can also be of considerable value.

If a course in rare book librarianship is offered, it is one instance in which to have it taught by a librarian who is practising in the field is probably the best method. In content it will of course treat of many of the matters dealt with in this book, and the student will acquire at least a theoretical understanding of some of the problems in using booksellers' catalogues, preparing exhibitions and so forth. Since so much of a rare book librarian's knowledge is acquired through familiarity with the materials, the more exposure that students can have to old books of all kinds the better. It is hopeless to try to organise a satisfactory programme of work without plenty of material for the students to handle. A collection purposefully built for this purpose, with representative examples of fine printing, early children's books, some three-deckers, a few yellowbacks and so on is of course excellent—but artificial. It lacks the organic coherence of a genuine collection built up over a period of time, with its mixture of important and unimportant, straightforward and complex, and containing some of the evidence of its own history as a collection. To work from a genuine library (like a parish library) as well as from specially chosen samples of books of different kinds, the books of which students will collate and catalogue, from which they can prepare special exhibitions, write descriptive notes and so forth, will be very useful.

This work will of course be supplemented by visits to restoration laboratories, to collections of special types of material, to exhibitions put on by rare book libraries, to meetings of bibliographical societies and the like. At the end of the programme the student will have handled a good many books from special collections and have learned from observation if not direct personal experience what is involved in the work. The student genuinely interested in this branch of librarianship will usually have shown himself a bookman already, and will be on the mailing lists for booksellers' catalogues and himself buying books in however small a way. The late A N L Munby's delightful recollections of book collecting in the 1930s(3) are but one instance of the way in which the bookman developes himself. Such interest can of course be fostered, and one of the most pleasurable aspects of working in a library school is to be able to discuss their new acquisitions with students, and at times to be able to help them to develop the research on books they have bought into notes for publication in book collecting or bibliographical journals.

An alternative to the programmes offered by library schools, not yet a practical one alas, has been suggested by Terry Belanger in a searching account of the Institute of Bibliography and Textual Criticism at Leeds.(4) In this account (a much more favourable one than my quotation implies) he suggests that programmes for higher degrees in bibliographical work should 'explore the relationships between bibliography and librarianship, especially rare book librarianship; between bibliography and the printing trades; between bibliography and the publishing trades, especially as regards graphic design and systematic bibliography. To train students in bibliography so that they may drive taxis is irresponsible.' To suggest that schools of librarianship may be bypassed is not likely to win much favour, but I believe that for the specialised work demanded in the rare book collection to have an intake of personnel with higher qualifications in bibliography (of the kind envisaged by Belanger) has much to commend it, albeit at the cost of a knowledge of the niceties of AACR or the provisions of the 1850 Public Libraries Act.

A route too little considered for developing the skills needed in the care of special collections is outside librarianship altogether: as an assistant in a firm of antiquarian booksellers. Several very distinguished rare book librarians in the United States have followed this route.

Nobody can deny that much of the best bibliographical scholarship is to be found in the staff of antiquarian dealers and book auction houses, but such a course has not often been pursued in Britain, although the career of the late A N L Munby has demonstrated how well it can work. For a good student to follow his time at library school with a year working in an antiquarian dealer's will give him exposure to a wider range of books of different periods and kinds, and the reference materials associated with them, than can be acquired otherwise. In view of the symbiotic relationship between the rare book library and the antiquarian market, such cross-fertilisation is to be encouraged. Nor is this an idle wish: at least some members of the antiquarian trade are very interested in such cooperation.

Another possibility, equally important, is for the library school graduate to seek attachment for a time in a large rare book library, where once more the novice will be exposed to a wider range of rare books and reference tools, and the expertise of the resident staff, than he could normally hope to gain in a first appointment. The fellowships offered by the Lilly Library at the University of Indiana are models of the kind of employment which is designed for the development of the rare book librarian.

The training of a librarian does not cease with the formal and informal programmes mentioned above. One of the joys of scholarly librarianship, like that of a straight academic career, is that it both permits and demands continued learning through research for the whole of one's professional career. And beyond: retirement is no barrier to continued work as the example of Victor Scholderer shows very clearly.

The librarian may well, in the course of his career, take other formal courses to round out his own education. The SCONUL courses on advanced bibliography organised at the Bodleian, are an instance of one such, while for the librarian working in a university to audit some of the advanced courses is not unusual. Some will take courses in binding and repair work; not to turn themselves into binders, of course (save as a hobby) but in order to increase their own competence in judging restoration and conservation problems.

Most of such continuing education will however be through the librarian's membership of bibliographic and other relevant bodies such as the Rare Books Group of the Library Association. At first, naturally, one will be purely a recipient of the benefits of attending lectures, seminars and so forth. Many of the benefits of these as of other professional meetings, will come less from the formal sessions than from the informal gatherings which go with them. As time goes by, it will be normal for the librarian to take a more active role, in reading papers to the societies or by taking office in them.

Such activities, though they will often call on the private time of the rare books librarian, should properly be regarded as part of his work in the library since they contribute to the publicity and use of the collections. It is normal for libraries to permit their staff time for attendence at meetings and (unhappily not in all instances) to provide funds for travelling expenses, conference fees and so forth.

The librarian will also have other committments to outside bodies. The friends of the library are not perhaps to be regarded as an outside group, and obviously the librarian's activities with the friends will be a part of his duties. But there are other bodies—local history societies, rotary clubs—whose activities may well impinge upon the library's role in the community, and in whose work the librarian may with advantage take interest.

Viewed from the aspect of a career, rare book librarianship today is at something of a crossroads. Changing concepts of the function of university and research libraries have long since destroyed the old pattern which found some favour in Victorian times, in which library posts could be regarded as suitable retreats for bibliographical scholarship. The rare book collection has to 'pay its way' and its librarian to make the case for providing services for which no justification would have been demanded a generation ago. At the same time, the man with antiquarian and bibliographic leanings and with sufficient private income to make salary and career prospects of relatively minor importance is (at any rate in Britain) an extinct breed.

Further, changes in the size and structure of academic and research libraries have often militated against the chance of progression for those whose interests tend towards work with rare books. Not only those, of course; James Thompson has drawn attention(5)

to the difficulties that the subject specialist has in a subject depart-
mentalised library in demonstrating such administrative competence
as will fit him for promotion to a university librarianship. But the
work of the rare book library, concerned as it is with relatively small
staffs and numbers of readers (and with almost none of its readership
at the undergraduate level or concerned with vocational training programmes) can give the rare books librarian the feeling that he is in a
backwater from which movement into the mainstream of library administration will be difficult. The opportunities which he has for play-
ing with some of the fashionable concepts of information retrieval,
computerised cataloguing and so forth though not entirely absent(6)
are less than in some other branches of library work, and he is likely to
be too busy with traditional and exacting standards of service to
regard some developments in librarianship as having much relevance
in the special collection. And he may therefore view with some dis-
quiet the qualities, both personal and professional, which will be demanded of the director of library services in a large academic
library—and also the duties which will be required of the incumbent
of such a post.

Despite this depressing picture, the future for the good rare books
librarian is far from gloomy. There is certainly greater mobility of
staff between research libraries than was the case even ten years ago,
while the great increase in the numbers of universities has led to the
development of many new special collections and a more general realisation of their importance for advanced research. In addition, one of
the useful side-effects of the great increase in the market values of antiquarian books has been a much deeper recognition that most libraries
will have *some* materials which need to be treated as rare; perhaps a
substantial collection of such books. A recent speaker at a meeting of
the Library Association Rare Books Group was by no means entirely
frivolous when he suggested that within a short period of time all
books printed before 1900 would be within the purview of the rare
book librarian. One cannot predict much wider opportunities in the
future than already exist for those whose sights are set on working
with incunabula or the Elizabethan dramatists, perhaps; but for those
whose professional pleasure will be in the type of work described in

the foregoing pages, and are prepared to work with nineteenth century science books, or little magazines of the 1940s, or with many other developing fields of special collections—for these there will be a continuing need in the libraries of the future.

References

1 This, if paper qualifications are to count at all, is really a minimal requirement. Since so much of the rare book librarian's work is concerned with giving assistance to those who are pushing back the frontiers of knowledge, it is obviously advantageous if the rare book librarian himself has the personal experience of what this involves, which can best be gained by working for a research degree.

2 Rollo G Silver 'The training of rare book librarians' *Library trends* vol 9 no 4, April 1961, pp 446–52.

3 A N L Munby 'Book collecting in Britain in the 1930s' *Times literary supplement* 11 May 1973.

4 In *Bibliography news* vol 3 no 1/2 Jan/Feb 1975, pp 2–4.

5 In his *An introduction to university library administration*, London, Bingley Hamdon, Conn, Linnet Books 1970 pp 33–4.

6 For example *Project LOC*; cf J W Jolliffe 'Project LOC and the "Fingerprint"' *Libri* vol 24 no 4, 1974, pp 240–8.

Bibliography

Periodicals of general relevance
AB bookman's weekly
American book collector
Bibliography newsletter
Book collector
The library
Library Association Rare Books Group newsletter
Library history
Papers of the Bibliographical Society of America
Private library
Restaurator

Books and articles

Adams, Frederick B: *The uses of provenance* Los Angeles, 1969.

Adams, Randolph G: 'Librarians as enemies of books' *Library Quarterly* vol 7, 1937, pp 317–31.

Archer, H Richard *ed: Rare book collections* Chicago, 1967 (ACRL Monograph 27)

Archer, H Richard: 'Special collections' *Library trends* vol 18 no 3, Jan 1970, pp 354–62.

The Bibliographical Society 1892–1942: studies in retrospect London, 1949.

Bodleian Library: *The Bodleian Library and its friends* Oxford, 1969.

Bodleian Library: *The John Johnson collection* Oxford, 1971.

Brewer, Frances: 'Friends of the library and other benefactors' *Library trends* vol 9 no 4, April 1961, pp 453–65.

Burnett, A D: 'Considerations on the support of antiquarian and other special collections in university libraries' *Journal of librarianship* vol 5 no 3, July 1973, pp 203–13.

Carter, John: *ABC for book collectors* 5th ed London, 1968.

Carter, John: 'Book auctions' *Library trends* vol 9 no 4, April 1961, pp

161

471–82.

Carter, John: *Books and book collectors* London, 1956.

Carter, John: *Taste and technique in book collecting* Reprinted with an epilogue. Pinner, 1970.

Connolly, Cyril: *100 modern books 1880–1950* London, 1965.

Cunha, Stanley: *Conservation of library materials* 2nd ed Metuchen, NJ, 1971.

Dunkin, Paul: *How to catalogue a rare book* Chicago, 1951.

Foxon, David: *Thoughts on the history and future of bibliographical description* Los Angeles, 1970.

Gardner, Anthony: 'The ethics of book repair' *The library* 5th series vol 9 no 3, 1954, pp 194–8.

Gaskell, Philip: *A new introduction to bibliography* Oxford, 1972.

Harvard University Library: *The Houghton Library 1942–1967; a selection of books and manuscripts* Cambridge, Mass, 1967.

Hertzberger, Menno *ed: A dictionary for the antiquarian book trade* Paris, 1956.

Hobbs, John C: *Local history and the library* London, 1962.

Hobson, Anthony: *Great libraries* London, 1970.

Horton, Carolyn: *Cleaning and preserving bindings and related material* 2nd ed Chicago, 1969 (LTP Publications, 16).

Library Association: *The care of books and documents* London, 1973 (L A Research Publication, 10).

Lehmann-Haupt, Helmut: 'On the rebinding of old books' in *Bookbinding in America: three essays* ed by H Lehmann-Haupt Rev ed New York, 1967.

McKerrow, R B: *An introduction to bibliography for literary students* Oxford, 1927.

Middleton, Bernard: *A history of English craft bookbinding technique* London, 1963.

Middleton, Bernard: *The restoration of leather bookbindings* Chicago, 1972. (LTP Publications, 18).

Muir, Percy *and* Carter, John, *eds: Printing and the mind of man* London, 1967.

Plumbe, W J: *The preservation of books in tropical and sub-tropical countries* Kuala Lumpur, 1964.

Quayle, Eric: *The collector's book of books* London, 1971.

Schad, Robert O: 'Friends of the Huntington Library' *Library trends* vol 5 no 4, April 1957, pp 483–8.

Silver, Rollo: 'The training of rare book librarians' *Library trends* vol 9 no 4, April 1961, pp 446–52.

Smith, R D: 'New approaches to preservation' *Library quarterly* vol 40 no 1, Jan 1970, pp 139–75.

Taubert, Sigfred: *Bibliopola; pictures and texts about the book trade* Hamburg, 1966.

Taylor, Archer: *Catalogues of rare books: a chapter in bibliographical history* Lawrence, 1958 (University of Kansas Publications, Library Series, 5).

Taylor, Archer: *Book catalogues: their varieties and uses* Chicago, 1957.

Thompson, G *ed: Museum climatology* London, 1967.

Thompson, Lawrence S: 'Facsimiles and the antiquarian trade' *Library trends* vol 9 no 4, April 1961, pp 437–45.

Tuttle, Helen Welch: 'Library-book trade relations' *Library trends* vol 18 no 3, Jan 1970, pp 398–411.

Wessel, Carl: 'Environmental factors affecting the permanence of library materials' *Library quarterly* vol 40 no 1, Jan 1970 pp 39–84.

Appendix

Extracts from the report *Book thefts from libraries* prepared by a working party of the Antiquarian Booksellers's Association and the Rare Books Group of the Library Association, 1972.

6 iv) Marking of books and documents

It is recommended that once a library or record office has acquired and accessioned a book or document, it should be so marked as to be quite obviously its property. This is particularly important when it is decided, as a matter of policy, to place books of value on open shelves. If, at some future date, it is legitimately sold, then this information should also be clearly marked in the volume or document. UNMARKED BOOKS, ONCE STOLEN, ARE RARELY RE-COVERABLE.

Marking therefore has a dual purpose. It acts as a deterrent to thieves and warns a prospective buyer that a book or document has been stolen. Four kinds of marking were considered:

i) Stamping with indelible ink; ii) Marking with invisible ink; iii) Embossing; iv) Perforation.

i) STAMPING WITH INDELIBLE INK Ink stamping is the traditional method to which librarians are accustomed and for which they normally have equipment. Provided that the stamp is well designed and not too large it is aesthetically acceptable and acts as a deterrent.

The objections to this method are: a) the ink used is by no means always indelible and, even if it is, the stamp can often be erased; it may remain obvious that a book once bore a stamp but it will probably be impossible to establish whose stamp it was. b) the method has been in use for so long and libraries have so frequently disposed of books *without cancelling their stamps* that most booksellers assume that a book with a library stamp has been deliberately discarded.

ii) MARKING WITH INVISIBLE INK This is feasible, and is of value in identifying stolen books, provided that would-be purchasers have a special lamp with which to detect it. There is, however, a very strong objection to having books marked in this way *only*. It has no deterrent value and indeed encourages thieves by suggesting that books are unmarked.

iii) EMBOSSING The use of embossed stamps is quite common in libraries and is aesthetically the most attractive method. But, it has the disadvantages of both the methods already described, in that like ink stamps it may be easy to remove and like invisible ink it may be so inconspicuous as not to act as a deterrent. The use of a small embossed stamp on a certain page of the text may, however, be useful for identification if a theft has taken place.

iv) PERFORATION This was suggested as a method which might be more widely adopted, using a code for the library, adopting a particular position on the page for the perforation, and supplying each library also with a cancellation die.

The great advantage of this method is that the perforations can go through a number of pages, and an expert paper repairer would be required to obliterate them. Even then, provided a uniform position was used for the perforation, the fact that the book had once been perforated would be obvious.

Perforation, however, seems likely to meet with opposition on aesthetic grounds, particularly as it is necessary to have letters and figures 3/16ths of an inch in height, if a perforating machine is to be used. With smaller perforations, the dies do not stand up to constant wear.

6 v) The working party came to the following conclusions:
a) All valuable books and documents should be marked in some way.
b) They should be seen to be marked.
c) The marking should be as difficult as possible to remove.

d) It is desirable to have some special, less obvious means of identification, such as the use of invisible ink, or a small inconspicuous
stamp or perforation on a specified page in the middle of the book,
which may not be noticed by a thief when removing more obvious
marks.

e) All valuable plates, maps or insertions in a book should also be
marked.

f) The marks must be cancelled, not obliterated if the book is to be disposed of.

g) It is the responsibility of a bookseller, or other purchaser, to check
with the library concerned, any book bearing an uncancelled mark of
ownership.

APPENDIX E: EMBOSSING

In Appendix C [evidence submitted by the British Museum Research
Laboratory and the Metropolitan Police Forensic Science Laboratory; not here reproduced] both Mr Baynes-Cope and Dr Seeley suggest that a combination of embossing, using a counter sunk die, and
suitable foils or pigments, may be the best solution to the marking
problem. There does not appear to be any simple machine available
at the moment which would carry this out, but the problem is being
investigated.

Index